Science

- Understanding science through literacy
- Investigative science skills
- The work of scientists

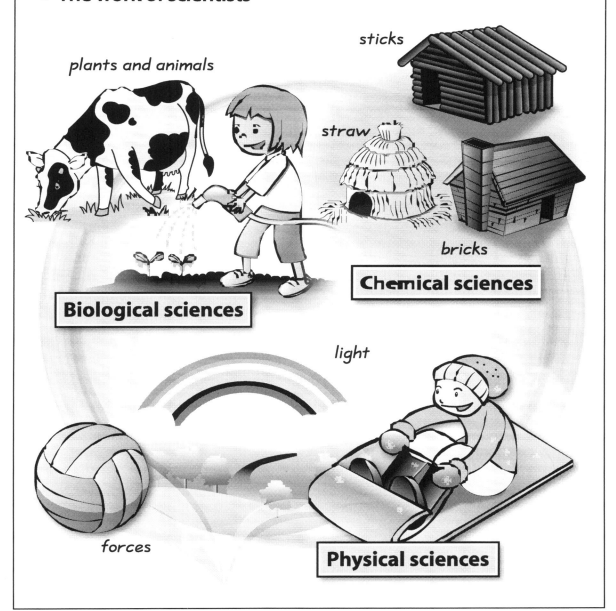

plants and animals

sticks

straw

bricks

Chemical sciences

Biological sciences

light

forces

Physical sciences

Science *Book 1 (Ages 5-6)*

Published by Prim-Ed Publishing® 2013
Copyright© R.I.C. Publications® 2011
ISBN 978-1-84654-577-1
PR– 6693

Titles in this series:
Science *Book 1 (Ages 5-6)*
Science *Book 2 (Ages 6-7)*
Science *Book 3 (Ages 7-8)*
Science *Book 4 (Ages 8-9)*
Science *Book 5 (Ages 9-10)*
Science *Book 6 (Ages 10+)*

Internet websites

In some cases, websites or specific URLs may be recommended. While these are checked and rechecked at the time of publication, the publisher has no control over any subsequent changes which may be made to webpages. It is *strongly* recommended that the class teacher checks *all* URLs before allowing pupils to access them.

View all pages online

Website: www.prim-ed.com

Foreword

Science – **Books 1-6** is a comprehensive series of science books for primary schools. Science literacy texts introduce concepts and are supported by practical hands-on activities, predominantly experiments.

Science investigative skills, and the requirement for pupils to work scientifically, underpin all topics.

Science is a complementary resource to the previously released Prim-Ed Publishing series, ***Primary science***.

Titles in this series are:
    Science Book 1 (Ages 5-6)
    Science Book 2 (Ages 6-7)
    Science Book 3 (Ages 7-8)
    Science Book 4 (Ages 8-9)
    Science Book 5 (Ages 9-10)
    Science Book 6 (Ages 10+)

Contents

Each book is divided into three or four sections, divided by shaded tabs down the side of each page. The four sections are: biological sciences, chemical sciences, Earth and space sciences and physical sciences.

Activities to enable pupils to appreciate the work of scientists are included in all sections.

Science investigative skills are included in all units. The skills utilised are listed on each teachers page.

Each section is divided into a number of four-page units, each covering a particular aspect and following a consistent format.

The four-page format of each unit consists of:

* a teachers page

* pupil page 1, which is a science literacy text about the concept with relevant diagrams or artwork

* pupil page 2, which includes comprehension questions about the literacy text

* pupil page 3, which involves a hands-on activity such as an experiment.

FOUR-PAGE FORMAT

Teachers page

The first page in each four-page format is a teachers page which provides the following information:

* A **shaded tab** gives the section.

* The **title** of the four-page unit is given.

* The **content focus** (the particular aspect of the unit covered in that set of four pages) is given.

* The **investigative skills** focus covered within the four pages is set out.

* **The lessons** provides information relating to implementing the lessons on the following pupil pages.

* **Background information,** which includes additional information for teacher and pupil use and useful websites relating to the topic of the section, expands on the unit.

* **Answers** and explanations are provided where appropriate for pupil pages 2 and 3 (the comprehension questions relating to the text and the final activity in the set of four pages).

* **Preparation** states any material or resources the teacher may need to collect to implement a lesson, or carry out an experiment or activity.

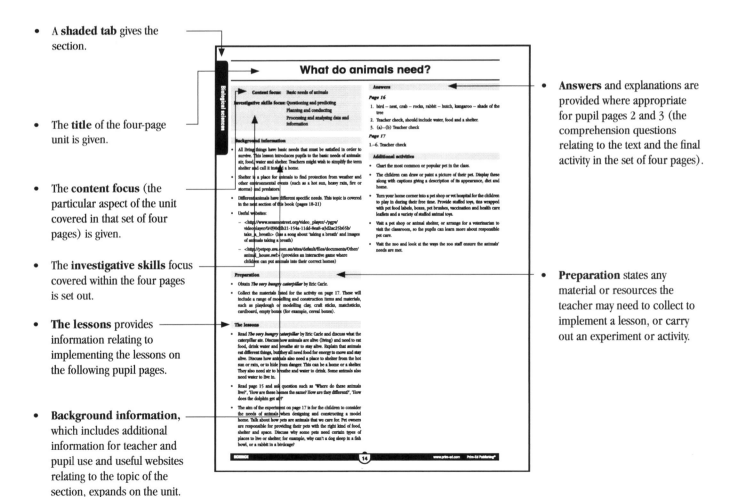

FOUR-PAGE FORMAT (continued)

Pupil page 1

The second page in the four-page format is a science literacy text which introduces the topic. This page provides the following information:

- A **shaded tab** down the side gives the section.

- The **title of the unit** is given. This is in the form of a question to incorporate science investigative skills and overarching ideas.

- The **science literacy text** is provided.

- Relevant **diagrams or artwork** enhance the text, or are used to assist pupil understanding of the concepts.

- **Teacher instructions** may be given

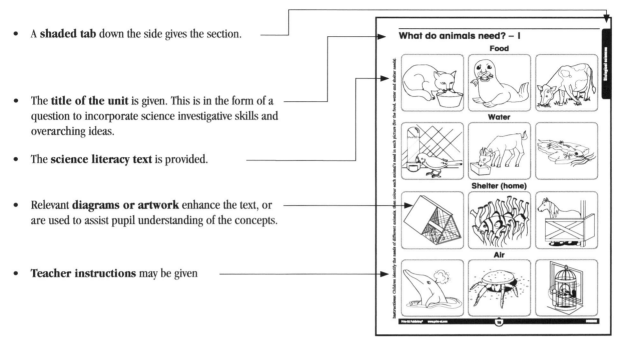

Pupil page 2

The second pupil page consists of a series of questions or activities relating to the literacy text. They aim to gauge pupil understanding of the concepts presented in the text.

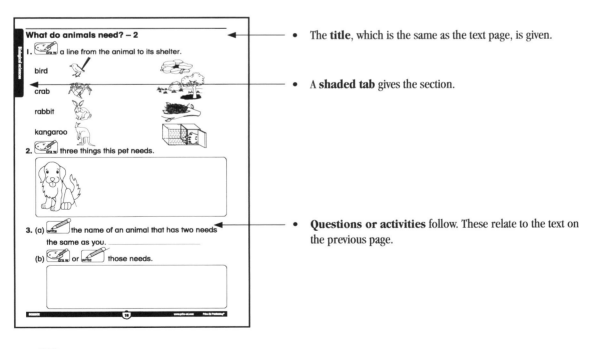

- The **title**, which is the same as the text page, is given.

- A **shaded tab** gives the section.

- **Questions or activities** follow. These relate to the text on the previous page.

Where relevant, a question relating to the work of scientists may be included as the final question on this page. This question is indicated by the icon shown to the left.

FOUR-PAGE FORMAT (continued)

Pupil page 3

The third pupil page provides a hands-on activity. It may be an experiment, art or craft activity, research activity or similar.

- A **shaded tab** gives the section.

- The **title** is given. This will be different from the previous two pages, but will be related to the concept focus of the unit.

- An **adapted procedure** for an experiment, craft activity or a research activity is given.

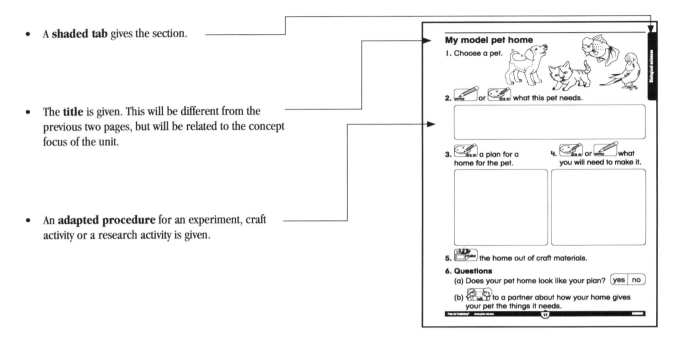

 ### The work of scientists units and questions

Some four-page units are related to the work of scientists.

Where the work of scientists questions occur within other units, they are indicated by the use of the icon. Explanations and answers relating to these questions are given on the appropriate teachers page.

Science investigative skills overview

Biological sciences					
PAGES	Questioning and predicting	Planning and conducting	Processing and analysing data and information	Evaluating	Communicating
2–5	✔	✔	✔	✔	✔
6–9	✔	✔	✔	✔	✔
10–13	✔	✔	✔	✔	✔
14–17	✔	✔	✔	✔	✔
18–21	✔	✔	✔	✔	✔
22–25	✔	✔	✔	✔	✔
26–29	✔	✔	✔	✔	✔
30–33	✔	✔	✔	✔	✔
34–37	✔	✔	✔	✔	✔
38–41	✔	✔	✔	✔	✔
42–45	✔	✔	✔	✔	✔

Chemical sciences					
PAGES	Questioning and predicting	Planning and conducting	Processing and analysing data and information	Evaluating	Communicating
46–49	✔	✔	✔	✔	✔
50–53	✔	✔	✔	✔	✔
54–57	✔	✔	✔	✔	✔
58–61	✔	✔	✔	✔	✔

Physical sciences					
PAGES	Questioning and predicting	Planning and conducting	Processing and analysing data and information	Evaluating	Communicating
62–65	✔	✔	✔	✔	✔
66–69	✔	✔	✔	✔	✔
70–73	✔	✔	✔	✔	✔
74–77	✔	✔	✔	✔	✔
78–81	✔	✔	✔	✔	✔

Report format

Title	
Classification *What is it?*	
Description	
Conclusion *What I think about it*	

Experiment format

Title	
Goal	
Materials	
Steps	
Results	
Conclusion	

England
Year 1 ~ Science

	pp2 – 5	pp6 – 9	pp10 – 13	pp14 – 17	pp18 – 21	pp22 – 25	pp26 – 29	pp30 – 33	pp34 – 37	pp38 – 41	pp42 – 45	pp46 – 49	pp50 – 53	pp54 – 57	pp58 – 61	pp62 – 65	pp66 – 69	pp70 – 73	pp74 – 77	pp78 – 81
Plants																				
• identify and name a variety of common plants						•														
• describe the basic structure of a variety of common plants including roots, stem, leaves and flowers						•	•	•												
Animals including humans																				
• identify and name a variety of common animals			•	•	•				•	•									•	
• describe and compare the structure of a variety of common animals and describe how they are suited to their environment			•		•				•	•										
• identify, name, draw and label the basic parts of the human body and say which part of the body is associated with each sense		•									•									
Light																				
• identify and name a variety of sources of light that we can see with our eyes, including electric lights, flames and the Sun																				•
• compare the variety of sources of light																				•

Curriculum links

England
Year 2 ~ Science

	pp2–5	pp6–9	pp10–13	pp14–17	pp18–21	pp22–25	pp26–29	pp30–33	pp34–37	pp38–41	pp42–45	pp46–49	pp50–53	pp54–57	pp58–61	pp62–65	pp66–69	pp70–73	pp74–77	pp78–81
All living things																				
• explain the differences between things that are living		•	•	•	•				•	•								•	•	
Plants																				
• describe how seeds and bulbs grow into mature plants							•													
• describe how plants need water, light and a suitable temperature to grow and stay healthy							•	•												
Animals including humans																				
• explain that animals including humans have offspring which grow into adults									•	•										
• explain the basic needs of animals, including humans, for survival	•			•	•				•	•										
Habitats																				
• identify that living things live in habitats to which they are particularly suited and describe how different habitats provide for the basic needs of different kinds of animals and plants, and how they depend on each other					•				•											
• identify and name a variety of plants and animals they study in a variety of habitats, including microhabitats				•	•	•			•											
Everyday materials																				
• distinguish between an object and the materials from which it is made													•	•						
• identify and name a variety of everyday materials, including wood, plastic, glass, metal, water, and rock												•	•	•						
• describe the simple physical properties of a variety of everyday materials												•	•	•	•					
• compare and group together a variety of everyday materials on the basis of their simple physical properties												•	•							
• find out how the shapes of solid objects made from some materials can be changed by squashing, bending, twisting and stretching													•							
Uses of everyday materials																				
• identify and compare the uses of a variety of everyday materials, including wood, metal, plastic, glass, brick/rock, and paper/cardboard													•	•		•				
Forces and motion																				
• describe how things move at different speeds, speed up and slow down																•	•			

Prim-Ed Publishing®   www.prim-ed.com

Curriculum links

Northern Ireland
Foundation Stage ~ The World Around Us

	pp2–5	pp6–9	pp10–13	pp14–17	pp18–21	pp22–25	pp26–29	pp30–33	pp34–37	pp38–41	pp42–45	pp46–49	pp50–53	pp54–57	pp58–61	pp62–65	pp66–69	pp70–73	pp74–77	pp78–81
Interdependence																				
• explore 'Who am I?' and 'What am I?'	•	•									•									
• explore 'Am I the same as everyone else?'	•	•									•									
• explore 'What else is living?'			•	•	•	•	•	•	•	•										
• explore 'How do living things survive?'	•			•	•	•	•	•	•	•	•									
Movement and energy																				
• explore 'How and why do things move?'																•	•	•	•	
• explore 'How do things work?'																•	•	•	•	
• explore 'Why do people and animals move?'																		•	•	•
• explore 'What sources of energy are in my world?'																				•
• explore 'How and why are they used?'																				
Progression																				
• show curiosity about living things, places, objects and materials in the environment	•	•	•	•	•	•	•	•	•	•		•	•	•	•	•	•	•		
• identify similarities and differences between living things, places, objects and materials	•	•	•		•	•	•	•	•	•		•	•	•		•	•	•	•	
• understand that some things change over time										•										
• understand that different materials behave in different ways, have different properties and can be used for different purposes												•	•	•	•					

Curriculum links

Republic of Ireland
Infant Classes ~ Science

Living things

	pp2–5	pp6–9	pp10–13	pp14–17	pp18–21	pp22–25	pp26–29	pp30–33	pp34–37	pp38–41	pp42–45	pp46–49	pp50–53	pp54–57	pp58–61	pp62–65	pp66–69	pp70–73	pp74–77	pp78–81
• identify parts of the male and female body		•																		
• recognise and measure physical similarities and differences between people		•																•		
• become aware that people have a variety of needs for growth (exercise, food, clothing, shelter)	•																			
• use all the senses to become aware of and explore environments											•	•								
• observe, discuss and identify a variety of plants and animals in different habitats and in the immediate environment			•		•	•	•	•	•	•										
• become aware of animals and plants of other environments			•	•	•				•	•									•	
• sort and group living things into sets			•		•	•			•	•									•	
• recognise and identify the external parts of living things			•			•		•	•											
• observe growth and change in some living things			•				•			•										
• explore conditions for growth of seeds							•													
• become aware that animals and plants undergo seasonal changes in appearance or behaviour										•										

Energy and forces

	pp2–5	pp6–9	pp10–13	pp14–17	pp18–21	pp22–25	pp26–29	pp30–33	pp34–37	pp38–41	pp42–45	pp46–49	pp50–53	pp54–57	pp58–61	pp62–65	pp66–69	pp70–73	pp74–77	pp78–81
• discuss differences between day and night, light and shade																				•
• explore, through informal activity with toys, forces such as pushing and pulling																•	•			
• investigate how forces act on objects																•	•	•		

Materials

	pp2–5	pp6–9	pp10–13	pp14–17	pp18–21	pp22–25	pp26–29	pp30–33	pp34–37	pp38–41	pp42–45	pp46–49	pp50–53	pp54–57	pp58–61	pp62–65	pp66–69	pp70–73	pp74–77	pp78–81
• observe and investigate a range of familiar materials in the immediate environment												•	•	•	•					
• describe and compare materials, noting the differences in the colour, shape and texture												•	•	•						
• know about some everyday uses of common materials												•	•	•						
• group materials according to certain criteria												•	•	•	•					
• investigate materials for different properties													•		•					
• identify some materials that are waterproof															•					

Curriculum links

Republic of Ireland
1st and 2nd Class ~ Science

Living things

Objective	pp2–5	pp6–9	pp10–13	pp14–17	pp18–21	pp22–25	pp26–29	pp30–33	pp34–37	pp38–41	pp42–45	pp46–49	pp50–53	pp54–57	pp58–61	pp62–65	pp66–69	pp70–73	pp74–77	pp78–81
recognise that all living things grow and change	•																			
name and identify external parts of the body and their associated senses		•																		
recognise and/or measure physical similarities and differences between individuals		•	•															•		
observe, identify and explore a variety of living things in local habitats and environments			•			•			•											
develop some awareness of plants and animals from wider environments			•		•				•											
group and sort living things into sets according to certain characteristics				•	•														•	
appreciate that living things have essential needs for growth					•		•													
recognise and describe the parts of some living things						•		•												
recognise that trees are plants						•														
investigate how plants respond to light							•													
understand that seasonal changes occur in living things and examine the changes in plant and animal life during the different seasons										•										
become familiar with the life cycles of common plants and animals										•										
become aware of the role of each sense in detecting information about the environment and in protecting the body											•									
use all the senses to become aware of and explore environments											•									

Energy and forces

Objective	pp2–5	pp6–9	pp10–13	pp14–17	pp18–21	pp22–25	pp26–29	pp30–33	pp34–37	pp38–41	pp42–45	pp46–49	pp50–53	pp54–57	pp58–61	pp62–65	pp66–69	pp70–73	pp74–77	pp78–81
explore how objects may be moved by pushing and pulling													•			•				
observe and investigate the movement of objects such as toys on various materials and surfaces																•	•			
investigate how forces act on objects																	•			
recognise that light comes from different sources																				•
recognise that the sun gives us heat and light, without which we could not survive																				•

Curriculum links

Republic of Ireland
1st and 2nd Class ~ Science *(continued)*

Materials	pp2 – 5	pp6 – 9	pp10 – 13	pp14 – 17	pp18 – 21	pp22 – 25	pp26 – 29	pp30 – 33	pp34 – 37	pp38 – 41	pp42 – 45	pp46 – 49	pp50 – 53	pp54 – 57	pp58 – 61	pp62 – 65	pp66 – 69	pp70 – 73	pp74 – 77	pp78 – 81
• identify and investigate a range of common materials used in the immediate environment												•	•							
• group materials according to their properties												•	•							
• describe and compare materials, noting the differences in colour, shape and texture													•							
• begin to explore how different materials may be used in the construction of homes suited to their environments														•						
• become aware of and investigate the suitability of different kinds of clothes for variations on temperature															•					

Curriculum links

Scotland
Early Stage ~ Sciences

	pp2 – 5	pp6 – 9	pp10 – 13	pp14 – 17	pp18 – 21	pp22 – 25	pp26 – 29	pp30 – 33	pp34 – 37	pp38 – 41	pp42 – 45	pp46 – 49	pp50 – 53	pp54 – 57	pp58 – 61	pp62 – 65	pp66 – 69	pp70 – 73	pp74 – 77	pp78 – 81
Planet Earth																				
• observe living things in the environment over time and become aware of how they depend on each other						•	•		•	•										
• grow plants, name their basic parts, and talk about how they grow and what I need to do to look after them						•	•	•												
• experience, use and describe a wide range of toys and common appliances, say 'what makes it go' and say what they do when they work																•	•			•
Forces																				
• through everyday experiences and play with a variety of toys and other objects, recognise simple types of forces and describe their effects																•	•	•	•	
Biological systems																				
• be aware of my growing body and learn the correct names for its different parts and how they work		•																		
• identify my senses and use them to explore the world around me											•	•								
• recognise that we have similarities and differences but are all unique	•		•	•	•															
Materials																				
• explore different materials and share reasoning for selecting materials for different purposes												•	•	•	•			•		

SCIENCE – Book 1   www.prim-ed.com · Prim-Ed Publishing®

Curriculum links

Wales

Foundation Stage ~ Knowledge and Understanding of the World

Myself and other living things

	pp2–5	pp6–9	pp10–13	pp14–17	pp18–21	pp22–25	pp26–29	pp30–33	pp34–37	pp38–41	pp42–45	pp46–49	pp50–53	pp54–57	pp58–61	pp62–65	pp66–69	pp70–73	pp74–77	pp78–81
• learn the names and uses of the main external parts of the human body and plants		•						•												
• observe differences between animals and plants, different animals, and different plants in order to group them			•	•	•	•	•		•										•	
• identify the similarities and differences between themselves and other children	•	•																•		
• learn about the senses that humans and other animals have and use to enable them to be aware of the world around them											•									
• identify some animals and plants that live in the outdoor environment				•	•	•			•	•										
• identify the effects the different seasons have on animals and plants										•										

Myself and non-living things

	pp2–5	pp6–9	pp10–13	pp14–17	pp18–21	pp22–25	pp26–29	pp30–33	pp34–37	pp38–41	pp42–45	pp46–49	pp50–53	pp54–57	pp58–61	pp62–65	pp66–69	pp70–73	pp74–77	pp78–81
• experiment with different everyday objects and use their senses to sort them into groups according to simple features												•	•	•	•	•	•			
• experiment with different everyday materials and use their senses to sort them into groups according to simple properties												•	•	•	•	•	•			
• develop an awareness of, and be able to distinguish between, made and natural materials													•	•						
• understand that light comes from a variety of sources, such as the Sun, and that darkness is the absence of light																				•

What are my needs?

Content focus:	The needs of humans
Investigative skill focus:	Questioning and predicting
	Planning and conducting
	Processing and analysing data and information
	Communicating

Background information

- Humans (and other living things) show the following features: they grow, move, reproduce, excrete, can sense and respond to stimuli in their environment, feed, and convert energy from the environment (food) for use.

- Humans and all living things have basic needs, without which they cannot survive. The basic needs of all living things are food, water, air and space. These needs differ slightly among animals, humans and plants, with humans also needing exercise, clothing, health care and love. In this section, only basic human needs are discussed.

- Useful website:
  - <http://www.ecoliteracy.org/downloads/needs-and-wants-activity> (Has colour images of a variety of needs and wants that can be downloaded and printed)

Preparation

- Obtain magazines, scissors, glue and coloured pencil crayons (including red and green pencil crayons).

- Collect the materials listed for the introduction (see below).

The lessons

- Place a toy (e.g. doll or teddy bear) where the children can see it. Ask them if the toy is alive. How do they know if it is alive or not? Ask the children what might happen to the toy if we don't give it food or drink, or store it in a box in the cupboard (nothing). Then choose one child to stand up and ask what might happen to that child if he or she doesn't get food or drink (he or she will get thirsty and hungry, and eventually become unwell and maybe die). Discuss how, because we are alive, we have to do and have certain things to stay alive and healthy. These things are called 'needs'. Ask the children to suggest some things they think they need to have to stay alive and healthy.

- Read page 3 with the children, ask them to suggest which need each picture represents. Remind them that without that need, they would become unhealthy. Ensure they understand the term 'shelter', and why shelter is a need. Encourage children to find the right word using the initial sound as a clue. For less able children, teachers might wish to write the first letter of the word so the children can find and write the rest of the word.

- Children complete page 4 independently. They will need magazines from which they can cut pictures of things they need.

- The aim of the activity on page 5 is for children to begin to understand that a person's needs change depending on different factors such as age, stage of development and the weather.

Answers

Page 3

Picture 1: food, 2: air, 3: water, 4: shelter, 5: clothes, 6: love.

Page 4

1. Teacher check
2. Fruit and vegetables and water are needs and should be coloured green. The toy and the balloon should be coloured red.
3. Teacher check

Page 5

Baby's needs: baby romper, baby hat, bottle of milk, baby food

Child's needs: a salad sandwich, glass of water, jumper and shoes

Additional activities

- In pairs, children can create different kinds of shelters using blocks or craft sticks and playdough.

- From magazines, cut pictures of foods that we need to eat (such as fruit, vegetables, cereals and bread) and those that we don't need but like nonetheless (sweets, chocolate, chips, soft drinks) and glue them onto separate sections of a sheet of paper.

- Cook a healthy snack in class or plan a healthy picnic that caters to everyone's needs.

- In pairs or in the home corner, children can act out how parents or carers give them the things they need at home.

- In pairs the children can decide on one other thing they think they need to add to the list on page 3, draw it and present it to the class, explaining their choice. Examples include exercise and medical care.

What are my needs? – 1

You eat, drink, breathe and grow. You are alive!

The pictures show some things you **need** to have, to stay healthy and alive.

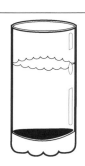

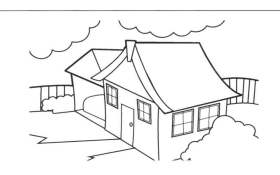

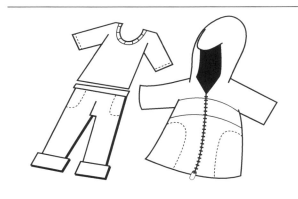

 the correct word under each picture.

| love | food | shelter | water | clothes | air |

What are my needs? – 2

1.  **2** pictures from magazines of things you need.

2. the things you **need** GREEN.

 the things you **don't need** RED.

  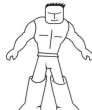 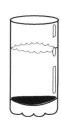

3. draw yourself getting **1** need.

Who needs what?

People's needs can be different.

 then the 'needs' pictures.

 them on the person they belong to.

Needs

What parts does my body have?

Content focus:	Basic visible features of the human body
Investigative skills focus:	Questioning and predicting
	Planning and conducting
	Processing and analysing data and information
	Evaluating
	Communicating

Background information

- The human body is made up of different parts, some of which can be seen and others (internal) that cannot. Each part helps us to do a different thing. This section introduces some basic external body parts. Teachers might also wish to discuss the functions of some of these parts, such as:

  - *hair*, which provides a barrier against the natural elements, helps regulate body temperature, and senses air movement and touch

  - *skin*, which provides a barrier against natural elements and microorganisms; produces vitamin D; regulates temperature; and senses touch, pain, heat or cold through nerve endings and receptors

  - *eyes*, which help us to see

  - a *mouth*, with which we eat, talk and taste

  - a *nose*, with which we smell

  - *ears*, with which we hear.

- Some useful websites:

  - <http://demo.onlineclub.iboard.co.uk/curriculum.htm#science-year1sci_yearyear1> has a selection of interactive labelling 'Me and us' activities.

  - <http://www.starfall.com/n/me/myBody/play.htm?f> has an interactive body labelling activity.

  - <http://www.crickweb.co.uk/ks1science.html>; scroll down to body parts and select from a number of age-appropriate body labelling interactive activities.

Preparation

- The pupils should learn familiar songs, action rhymes and dances involving body parts which they can perform.

- If possible, obtain a full-length mirror for the pupils to use to look at their bodies. Alternatively, small mirrors can be used to closely examine faces and find the colour of eyes, shape of eyebrows etc.

The lessons

- Read a book about body parts or look at a labelled chart of the body with the pupils. Discuss how people's bodies have parts that do different things. Discuss how these different parts help us live and find out about the world and do the things we want to do.

- Briefly discuss which things the different body parts help us do.

- Read page 7 with the pupils and ask them to point to the word and body part as you read each.

- The aim of the activity on page 9 is for pupils to record information about similar and different external parts of their body. Upon completion of the activity, ask the pupils what was the same or different. Ask what body parts might change as they get older. Will their hair be the same colour or different? How might their feet change? Which body parts will stay the same?

Answers

Page 8

1. Each body part helps the person do something.

2. Answers will vary but should include: hair, eyebrow, eye, ear, nose, mouth, chin.

3. (a) 2 arms, 2 legs, 2 feet, 2 eyes, 2 ears, 2 eyebrows, 2 hands, 2 ankles, 2 shoulders, 2 elbows, 2 knees, 10 fingers, 10 toes, 1 mouth, 1 chin, 1 head, 1 nose, 1 neck

   (b)–(d) Teacher check

4. Answers will vary but may include: hair, fingernails and toenails.

5. Answers will vary but may include: chest, back, thigh, cheek, teeth, waist, bottom, stomach, lips, forehead, heel, fingernails, toenails, thumb.

Page 9

Teacher check

What parts does my body have? – I

Read the text.

People have many body parts on the outside. Each part helps the person to do something. Written below are some names of body parts.

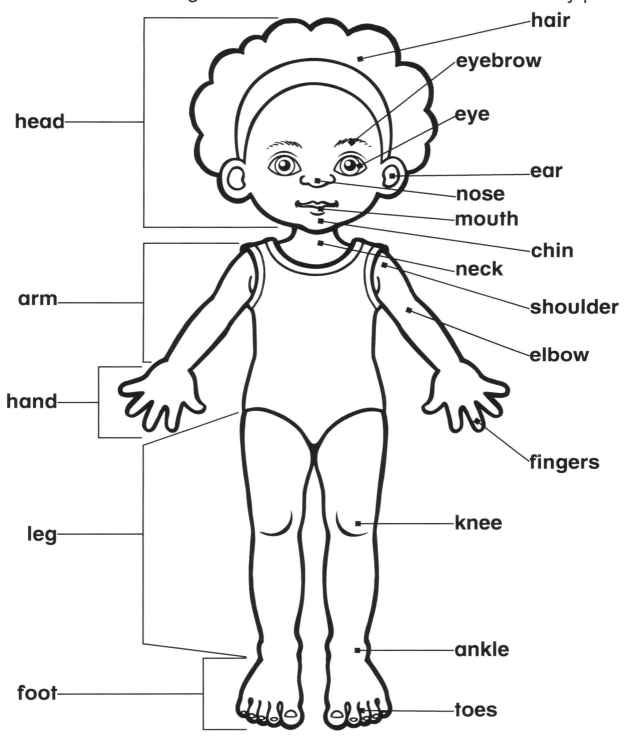

Do you know what each body part does?
Can you think of any other body parts on the outside?

What parts does my body have? – 2

Use the text and diagram on page 7 to complete the following.

1. What are body parts for? Complete the sentence.

   Each body part helps the person …

   _____.

2. Write the name of four body parts on the head.

   - _____   - _____

   - _____   - _____

3. (a) Write how many of each body part there are altogether.

☐ arms	☐ legs	☐ feet
☐ eyes	☐ ears	☐ eyebrows
☐ hands	☐ ankles	☐ shoulders
☐ elbows	☐ knees	☐ fingers
☐ toes	☐ mouth	☐ chin
☐ head	☐ nose	☐ neck

   (b) Tick the ones there are two of using red pencil.

   (c) Tick the ones there are ten of using blue pencil.

   (d) Tick the ones there is one of using yellow pencil.

4. Name a body part that grows that must be cut regularly.

   _____

5. Write another body part, not on the diagram, that can be seen.

   _____

Investigating our bodies

Draw or write in the table to compare yourself to a friend.

	Myself	My friend
Hair colour		
Eye colour		
Skin colour		
Nose shape		
Eye shape		
Mouth shape		
Chin shape		

Can animals be different?

<table>
<tr><td>Content focus:</td><td>There are different kinds of animals</td></tr>
<tr><td></td><td>Animals come in different shapes and sizes</td></tr>
<tr><td></td><td>Animals have babies</td></tr>
<tr><td>Investigative skills focus:</td><td>Questioning and predicting</td></tr>
<tr><td></td><td>Planning and conducting</td></tr>
<tr><td></td><td>Processing and analysing data and information</td></tr>
<tr><td></td><td>Communicating</td></tr>
</table>

Background information

- An animal is a living organism that can move on its own, has sensation and ingests food.

- There are many kinds of animals, each with numerous features. Animals sharing certain features can be grouped or sorted into categories. For example, they may be aquatic creatures, have four legs, be wild, be pets, or be found at a farm. Animals can also be placed into subcategories such as birds, mammals, reptiles or amphibians.

- Animals are born, grow and change in different ways before dying. Teachers might wish to further investigate the changes occurring during a particular animal's life cycle.

- Useful websites:

  – <http://bogglesworldesl.com/animal_body_parts.htm> (offers flash cards that can be downloaded, showing animals with a variety of different body parts)

  – <http://kids.nationalgeographic.com/kids/animals/creaturefeature/> (has a large range of animals in different categories that pupils can click on to find out more about)

Preparation

- Cut, copy and laminate the pictures on page 11 prior to the lesson if desired.

- Collect the materials listed for the experiment on page 13. You will need large and small circles cut from different animal print fabrics, A4 sheets of coloured card, glue and a range of materials for decorating the animals such as craft eyes, buttons, cotton wool balls, feathers, cord, foil, rice or seeds, and pipe-cleaners.

The lessons

- Say the 'At the zoo' rhyme:

'At the zoo I saw a bear, It had short, dark, furry hair (pretend to walk like a bear), I saw a kangaroo hopping round, Its big feet pushed it high off the ground (pretend to be a jumping kangaroo), The cheeky monkeys made me laugh And I saw a big, long-necked giraffe. I saw an elephant, big and strong, It's trunk was very, very long! But my favourite animal at the zoo Was the crocodile – how about you?'

- Discuss how there are many different kinds of animals. They have different body parts, do different things and live in different places. Some animals we keep as pets, others we keep at farms and the rest are wild. Animals are living things that eat, grow and have babies.

- The activity on page 11 can be done in a number of ways. The pictures can be copied onto card and laminated for use in sorting activities (make a group of animals that might live in a zoo/that have fur/that can be pets/that have sharp teeth/that are big or small), or as games (place the cards face down, children turn over 2 cards and try to find a similar feature such as 'They both have fur', or as a game like 'fish' where children take 5 cards and one at a time ask another child a question to find a pair, such as 'Do you have an animal with scales?'

- The aim of the activity on page 13 is for pupils to create an imaginary animal then describe it using different scientific terms.

Answers

Page 11

The animals can be sorted in different ways.

Page 12

1. Teacher check
2. home – cat: farm – sheep: zoo – snake
3. sheep – lamb: cow – calf: lion – cub: dog – puppy

Page 13

Teacher check

Additional activities

- With children in small groups, ask each child to draw a different animal body part (without showing anyone else which animal they have chosen); for example, one child draws a head, another a tail, another draws wings. When they have finished, assemble the animal and create an interesting name for it.

- Play 'pin the (tail, nose, horns, eyes) on the animal'. Draw an animal on a large sheet of paper or card; the children close their eyes and try to pin the part in the right spot.

- Two children sit in front of the group with an animal picture above them (or fastened to a headband) so they do not know what it is. They ask questions with yes or no answers, such as 'Do I have feathers?' or 'Am I a good swimmer?' to try to work out which animal they are.

- Play charades with the children pretending to be different animals.

Can animals be different? – I

Instructions: Children cut out then sort the animals in different ways; e.g based on their features, the type of animal they are or the environment they live in.

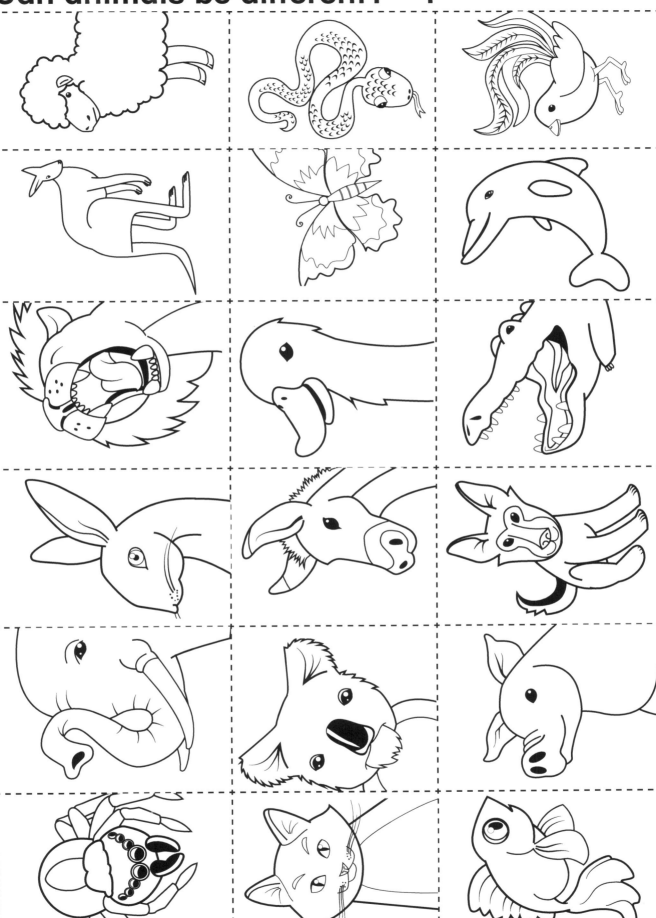

Can animals be different? – 2

1.  an animal that is:

big	small	tiny

2.  a line to the animal you can see:

in a home •

on a farm •

in a zoo •

3.  out the babies.  them with their parent.

sheep	cow	lion	dog

cub   lamb   calf   puppy

Creative circle creatures

What you need:

- I large and I small circle of animal print fabric
- decorations (e.g. pipe-cleaners, buttons, cotton wool balls)
- glue • A4 coloured card

What to do:

I.  glue the large fabric circle on the coloured card.

2. glue the smaller circle on top of it.

3. Give your creature features such as teeth, horns, eyes, ears, legs or wings.

4. Fill in the table.

What is your animal called?	
Where does it live?	
What does it eat?	
What can it do?	

5.  draw your creature on the back of the page.

What do animals need?

<table>
<tr><td>Content focus:</td><td>Basic needs of animals</td></tr>
<tr><td>Investigative skills focus:</td><td>Questioning and predicting</td></tr>
<tr><td></td><td>Planning and conducting</td></tr>
<tr><td></td><td>Processing and analysing data and information</td></tr>
</table>

Background information

- All living things have basic needs that must be satisfied in order to survive. This lesson introduces pupils to the basic needs of animals: air, food, water and shelter. Teachers might wish to simplify the term shelter and call it instead a home.

- Shelter is a place for animals to find protection from weather and other environmental events (such as a hot sun, heavy rain, fire or storms) and predators.

- Different animals have different specific needs. This topic is covered in the next section of this book (pages 18-21)

- Useful websites:

  – <http://www.sesamestreet.org/video_player/-/pgpv/ videoplayer/0/d90ddb21-154a-11dd-8ea8-a3d2ac25b65b/ take_a_breath> (has a song about 'taking a breath' and images of animals taking a breath)

  – <http://petpep.ava.com.au/sites/default/files/documents/Other/ animal_house.swf> (provides an interactive game where children can put animals into their correct homes)

Preparation

- Obtain *The very hungry caterpillar* by Eric Carle.

- Collect the materials listed for the activity on page 17. These will include a range of modelling and construction items and materials, such as playdough or modelling clay, craft sticks, matchsticks, cardboard, empty boxes (for example, cereal boxes).

The lessons

- Read *The very hungry caterpillar* by Eric Carle and discuss what the caterpillar ate. Discuss how animals are alive (living) and need to eat food, drink water and breathe air to stay alive. Explain that animals eat different things, but they all need food for energy to move and stay alive. Discuss how animals also need a place to shelter from the hot sun or rain, or to hide from danger. This can be a home or a shelter. They also need air to breathe and water to drink. Some animals also need water to live in.

- Read page 15 and ask question such as 'Where do these animals live?', 'How are these homes the same? How are they different?', 'How does the dolphin get air?'

- The aim of the experiment on page 17 is for the children to consider the needs of animals when designing and constructing a model home. Talk about how pets are animals that we care for. Pet owners are responsible for providing their pets with the right kind of food, shelter and space. Discuss why some pets need certain types of places to live or shelter; for example, why can't a dog sleep in a fish bowl, or a rabbit in a birdcage?

Answers

Page 16

1. bird – nest, crab – rocks, rabbit – hutch, kangaroo – shade of the tree

2. Teacher check, should include water, food and a shelter.

3. (a)–(b) Teacher check

Page 17

1.–6. Teacher check

Additional activities

- Chart the most common or popular pet in the class.

- The children can draw or paint a picture of their pet. Display these along with captions giving a description of its appearance, diet and home.

- Turn your home corner into a pet shop or vet hospital for the children to play in during their free time. Provide stuffed toys, tins wrapped with pet food labels, boxes, pet brushes, vaccination and health care leaflets and a variety of stuffed animal toys.

- Visit a pet shop or animal shelter, or arrange for a veterinarian to visit the classroom, so the pupils can learn more about responsible pet care.

- Visit the zoo and look at the ways the zoo staff ensure the animals' needs are met.

What do animals need? – I

Biological sciences

Food

Water

  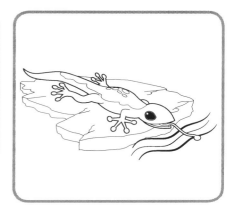

Shelter (home)

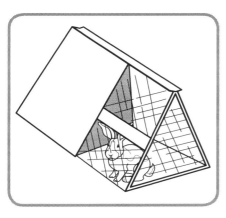 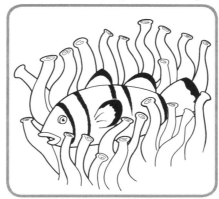 

Air

Instructions: Children identify the needs of different animals, then colour each animal's need in each picture (for the food, water and shelter needs).

What do animals need? – 2

1.  a line from the animal to its shelter.

bird

crab

rabbit

kangaroo

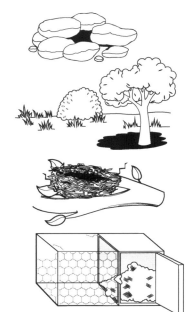

2. draw three things this pet needs.

3. (a) write the name of an animal that has two needs

the same as you. _____

(b) draw or write those needs.

My model pet home

1. Choose a pet.

2. [write] or [draw] what this pet needs.

3. [draw] a plan for a home for the pet.

4. [draw] or [write] what you will need to make it.

5. [make] the home out of craft materials.

6. Questions

(a) Does your pet home look like your plan?   [yes | no]

(b) [talk] to a partner about how your home gives your pet the things it needs.

Do all animals have the same needs?

Content focus:	Animals in different situations have different needs
Investigative skills focus:	Questioning and predicting
	Planning and conducting
	Processing and analysing data and information
	Communicating

Background information

- While animals have the same basic needs, the specifics of their diets, habitats and other needs vary. For example, all animals eat but most animals are adapted to eat specific kinds of food. All animals need water as it is essential for transporting nutrients and chemicals around their bodies, but some animals need far more than others and some also need water to live in.

- Pets, zoo and farm animals need people to help them get their needs, while animals that live in the wild get their needs themselves. Generally, these wild animals require more space to forage and obtain food.

- Snails are animals that can be quite easily found in the local environment and observed in the classroom.

- Useful website:
  - <http://www.brainpopjr.com/health/beresponsible/ caringforpets/grownups.weml> (has information and activity ideas around the theme of caring for different animals)

Preparation

- Collect the materials listed for the experiment on page 21.

The lessons

- If possible, complete these pages after doing pages 14–17. Ensure that children understand the basic needs that all animals share.

- Introduce the lesson with a rhyme, such as

  'Snails eat grass, horses do too,

  but lions eat meat, how about you?

  Birds live in a nest, wasps do too,

  but worms live underground, how about you?

  Fish swim in the water, turtles do too,

  but cats live on land, how about you?

  Goldfish need feeding, dogs do too,

  but emus find their own food, how about you?'

- Discuss how animals in different situations can have different needs. Read page 19 with the children and ask them to tell you some of the different foods and shelters, and space requirements, animals can have. Ask them to describe the needs of any pets they may have and compare those needs.

- The aim of the experiment on page 21 is for the pupils to predict, then observe and record which foods snails eat. Paper is a good item to test because the children might not guess correctly that snails will eat paper. The snails can be kept in a terrarium, aquarium, or large plastic container. The top should be securely covered with a breathable material (such as flyscreen material or nylon stocking). It might be advisable to take a picture of the foods in place in the box before the snails go in, and then another picture a few hours later (or overnight). Comparing the two pictures side by side will help the children to determine how much of each food the snails have eaten. After the activity, ask questions such as 'Were you surprised by anything the snails ate?', 'Which foods do you think the snails like best?', 'Were your guesses right or wrong?' Some teachers might wish to cut the chart from the page, enlarge it and give each child a copy of the chart only.

Answers

Page 20

1. No, fish and kangaroos don't need the same food.

2. Fox: one of the following; trees or burrow, insects, birds, rabbits, mice or water. Chicken: one of the following: water, grain and insects, a coop or shed.

3. Teacher check as answers will vary. Children could indicate that both animals need water, or that they both eat flies and other small insects.

4. Meat to eat: lion and eagle. Water to live in: jellyfish and clown fish. (both of these also eat 'meat' so they could be put into the first box). Lots of space: elephant and horse.

Page 21

1.–5. Teacher check

Additional activities

- Turn different walls or display boards in your classroom into different habitats. The children can draw animals to put in these habitats, along with shelters and food and water sources for them.

- Find and cut pictures of different habitats and pictures of different animals in magazines. The children can match the animals to their habitats.

- Get a class pet such as a goldfish. Find out what your pet needs together and make a roster of children to care for the pet.

- Visit a local zoo, wildlife park, farm, wetland area, aquarium or natural history museum to find out more about different animals and their needs.

Do all animals have the same needs? – I

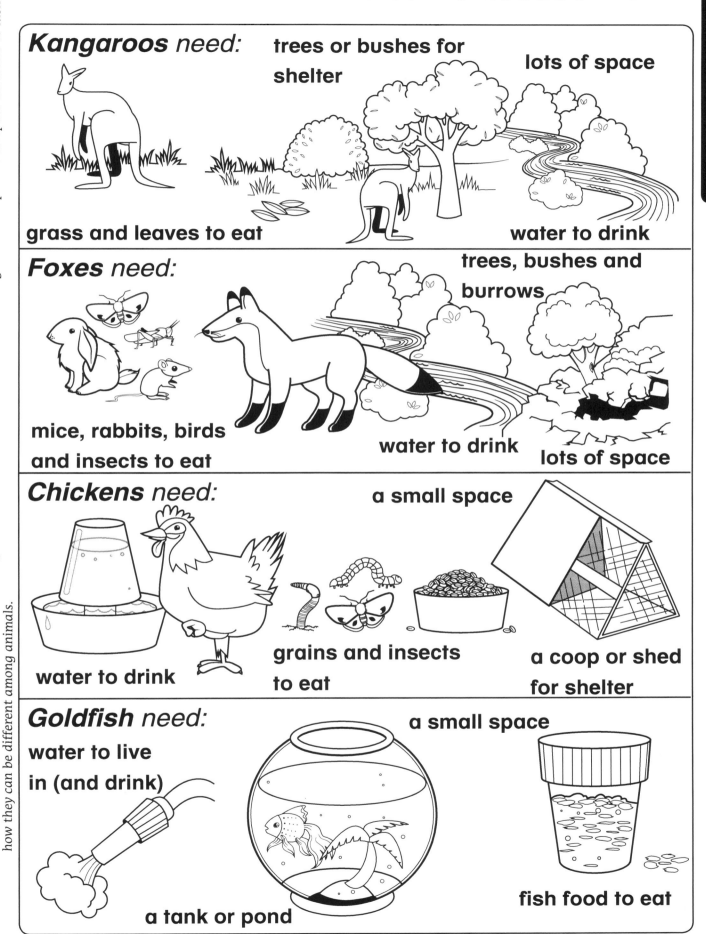

Kangaroos *need:*

trees or bushes for shelter

lots of space

grass and leaves to eat

water to drink

Foxes *need:*

trees, bushes and burrows

mice, rabbits, birds and insects to eat

water to drink

lots of space

Chickens *need:*

a small space

water to drink

grains and insects to eat

a coop or shed for shelter

Goldfish *need:*

water to live in (and drink)

a small space

a tank or pond

fish food to eat

Biological sciences

Instructions: Children colour the needs in different colours—e.g. food needs in brown and the shelter needs in green—to help them compare the needs to identify how they can be different among animals.

Do all animals have the same needs? – 2

1. Do fish and kangaroos need the same food? | yes | no |

2. [draw] a need for each animal.

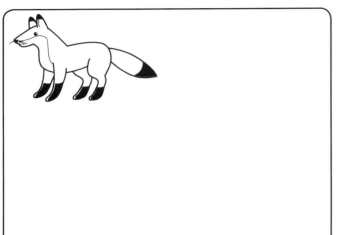

3. [write] a need these two animals share.

4. [cut] and sort the animals.

other animals (meat) to eat	water to live in	lots of space

What food will snails eat?

Materials:

• snails • large containers (with a cover) • five food items (e.g. choose five from lettuce, apple, sliced meat, paper, leaves, flour, sticky tape)

Steps:

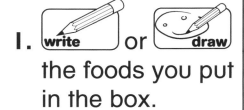

1. write or draw the foods you put in the box.

2. Put a ✔ for the foods you think the snails will eat and an ✖ for those you think they won't.

3. Put the snails in the box. After a few hours, look to see which foods the snails ate.

4. Finish the chart with a ✔ if the snails ate the food or a ✖ if they didn't.

Foods in the box	Will the snails eat it? (guess)	Did the snails eat it?

5. talk about what was hard or easy about this experiment.

What is a plant?

Content focus:	Basic features of plants
Investigative skills focus:	Questioning and predicting
	Planning and conducting
	Processing and analysing data and information
	Communicating

Background information

- Plants are living organisms. Trees, flowers, herbs, bushes, grasses, vines and ferns are examples of plants.

- Despite having plant-like characteristics, most algae, (including seaweed) and fungi, including mushrooms, toadstools and mildew, are not considered true plants.

- Most plants use the energy in sunlight to convert carbon dioxide from the atmosphere, plus water, into simple sugars.

- There are different types of plants, including grasses, fruit-bearing plants and grains.

- Useful websites:

  - <http://www.angelfire.com/la/kinderthemes/pfingerplays.html> (a site containing a number of plant-themed songs and fingerplays)

  - <http://www.crickweb.co.uk/ks1science.html> (has an interactive activity where the children can label the four main parts of a plant)

Preparation

- Obtain some different plants to bring in to the class (e.g. a small fern, a flowering plant, a cactus or other succulent, herbs).

- Collect the materials listed for the experiment on page 25.

The lessons

- If possible, bring in a number of different plants and set them up on a table with magnifying glasses. Allow the children to look at, investigate, smell and feel the plants. Ask the children to share their observations. What colours can they see? What shapes? Which plants smelled nice? Which ones had smooth parts?

- Explain that there are all sorts of different plants. Read the sheet with the children and ask them to draw a line with a pencil or their finger to the picture as you read the word. After reading the plant parts, the children can point to the corresponding parts in the plants in the class or in the pictures on the page.

- The aim of the experiment on page 25 is for the children to explore their local environment and observe the different types of plants they see. They need to sort the plants they find into categories, record their observations and compare their observations with others. Teachers will need to demonstrate taking a rubbing of a leaf before the activity. Put the leaf (vein side up) on the table (or other hard surface), put the paper in place on top and rub gently over it with the flat side of a crayon.

Answers

Page 24

1.–3. Teacher check

4. small plant with flowers – petunia: small plant with a part we eat – tomato plant: big plant with flowers – flowering gum: big plant with a part we eat – banana tree.

Page 25

1.–4. Teacher check

Additional activities

- Plant a seed (e.g sunflower seed) in a ziplock bag with a damp paper towel. Tape the bags to a window and observe as they germinate and grow.

- Visit a nursery, botanical garden or local gardens and look at different plants, especially local plants. Do direct observational drawings of interesting plants. After the visit, the children can graph their favourite flowers or plants.

- Provide the children with a variety of seeds to sort and classify, or to create artworks with.

- Grow carrot tops. Find carrots with some sign of a shoot on the top. Cut a 2cm section from the top of the carrot and place this on a small plate with a small amount of water in it. Leave in a well-lit place (e.g. a windowsill) and keep the water topped up. In a few days leaves should start to grow on the top of the carrot.

- Grow, smell and taste some different herbs.

- Print with vegetables, fruits, lettuce and cabbage leaves.

- Dry (press) flowers.

- Go into the school grounds or garden and play 'eye spy with my little eye' a plant that … (is small, tall, green, has lots of leaves, has flowers, smells nice).

- The children can cut and sort pictures of different plants from magazines.

What is a plant? – I

A tree is a plant.

Grass is a plant.

A vine is a plant.

A carrot is a plant.

A bush is a plant.

Most plants have:

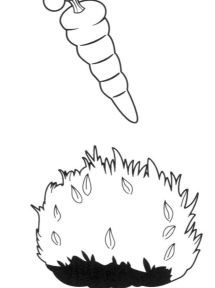

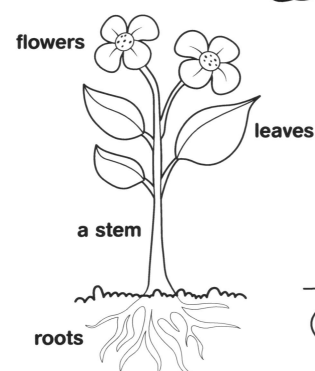

flowers

leaves

a stem

roots

Most plants grow from a seed.

Instructions: Children draw a line from the name of the plant to its picture as the teacher reads.

What is a plant? – 2

1.  around. a plant you can see.

2. a line from each word to the plant part.

flower

stem

leaf

3. Circle a plant that smells nice.

4.  , sort and glue the plants into the chart.

	with flowers	with a part we eat
small plant		
big plant		

Plants around me

1. Go outside. Tally the types of plant you find. Fill in the last column with a different type of plant you find.

	Trees	Bushes	Flowers	Grasses	
Tally **(ĻĦŤ, ĻĦŤ)**					

2.  **draw** and **colour** two plants you found.

3. Find a leaf.

Take a rubbing.

4. **talk** to a friend about what he or she found outside. Did you have the same results?

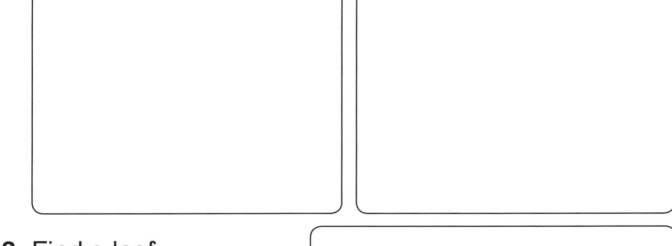

What do plants need?

Content focus:	Basic needs of plants
	Comparing the needs of different plants, and plants and animals
Investigative skills focus:	Questioning and predicting
	Planning and conducting
	Processing and analysing data and information
	Communicating

Background information

- The basic needs of plants are air (atmospheric carbon dioxide is converted into simple sugars using the energy in sunlight during photosynthesis), water (with different plants having their own water requirements, some needing dry conditions and others needing a consistent supply of moisture), sunlight (the source of energy for plants to prepare their food through photosynthesis) and soil (with the appropriate humidity and balance of nutrients and minerals).

- The temperature of the soil as well as surrounding atmosphere also greatly influences plant growth, with different plant species requiring different atmospheric temperatures.

- Plants in the garden at home, or inside homes, and plants in the wild have different needs. Plants at home often have to be watered, fertilised and pruned, while plants in the wild don't require this kind of care.

- Useful website:
  - <http://www.woodlands-junior.kent.sch.uk/revision/Science/living/plants.html> (has information on plants and links to games and other sites)

Preparation

- Collect the materials listed for the experiment on page 29.

The lessons

- If possible, complete pages 18–21 and 22–25 before doing these pages.

- Say a rhyme with the class, such as 'I have a little garden' (I have a little garden, a garden of my own, And every day I water there the seeds that I have sown. I love my little garden, and tend it with such care, You will not find a faded leaf or blighted blossom there).

- If possible, show the children a healthy pot plant and one that is either unhealthy or dead. Discuss how plants, like people and animals, need to have certain things to stay alive. Ask the children to suggest things they think a plant might need. Discuss these suggestions and how we use this knowledge of what plants need to care for plants in our homes and gardens.

- Read page 27 with the children. After reading once, read again and allow the children to draw a line from the part you are reading to the matching picture.

- The aim of the experiment on page 29 is for the children to create a grass head creature that they will need to consider the needs of in order for it to grow.

Answers

Page 28

1. Teacher check
2. The roots should be circled.
3. Children should write or draw a picture to represent either water or air.
4. Plant: water (rain), sun, soil and air.
   Dog: water, air, food and a shelter (kennel).

Page 29

1. Children should write or draw air, water and sunlight.
2. Teacher check. Children should indicate that they will need to put their grass head in a sunny position, in a place where it will get air, and that they will need to give it water.

Additional activities

- Grow other plants, such as bean plants, from seed, or grow a class plant. Track the growth of these plants each week. At the beginning of each week, have pupils draw what they think the plant will look like by the end of the week, and compare their predictions with the actual results.

- Plant a herb or vegetable garden in the school grounds. The children can help to choose the right position and plants, and take turns to help care for the plants they grow.

- Look at the types of plants that grow naturally in the local environment. Find out how these plants survive.

- Investigate plants that grow in extreme environments, such as in the desert or in very cold places.

- Experiment with plant needs by removing one need, such as sunlight or water, and observing what happens to the plant.

- Give the children a straw and a cup of water. Tell them they are the plants and the straws are the roots that suck up the water for the plant to use.

- Read *The little red hen* and discuss how the hen cared for her seeds and helped them turn into wheat plants. Discuss farmers, gardeners and other people who work to look after plants.

What do plants need? – I

Animals and people need to eat food to grow.

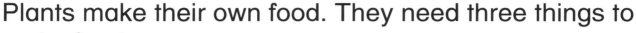

Plants don't.

Plants make their own food. They need three things to make food:

sunlight

air

and **water**.

Plants need **soil**.

Roots take water and **nutrients** from the soil.

Some plants need people to give them water and nutrients.

Some plants get their own nutrients.

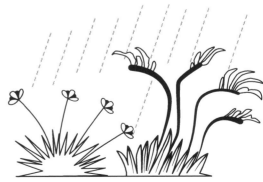

 out caring for plants in your garden.

What do plants need? – 2

1. **write** the needs in the right place.

| water |
| sunlight |
| air |
| soil |

2. (Circle) the plant part that takes water from the soil.

   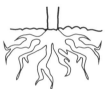

3. **draw** or **write** one thing plants and animals both need.

4. **cut** and sort the needs.

    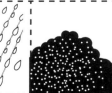

Make a grass-head!

Materials:

- plastic or polystyrene cup
- leg of a pair of stockings
- I cup of sawdust or potting mix   • elastic bands
- decorating materials (e.g. felt, markers, craft eyes)
- I teaspoonful of grass seeds

What to do (tick each step as you do it).

☐ **I.** Put grass seeds into the toe of the stockings.

☐ **2.** Put potting mix into the stocking.

☐ **3.** Tie a knot in the open end.

☐ **4.** Put it in the cup, knot end down.

☐ **5.** Decorate a face.

Questions

I. What does your grass-head need to grow?

2. How will you make sure it gets these needs?

What are the main parts of a plant?

Content focus:	Main features of plants and their functions
Investigative skills focus:	Questioning and predicting
	Planning and conducting
	Processing and analysing data and information
	Evaluating
	Communicating

Background information

- This unit covers the basic parts of flowering plants which are described on page 31. Further information about stems, the focus of the experiment on page 33, includes that they contain vascular tissue. Tubes called 'xylem' suck up water and tubes called 'phloem' suck up nutrients. They both act like tiny straws.

- Blue food colouring produces the most vibrant leaf colour in the experiment on page 33. White carnations are another effective way of showing pupils how water travels via the stem. Place a cut flower into water containing food colouring and the petals will change colour.

- Some useful websites:

  - visit <http://www.hhmi.org/coolscience/forkids/vegquiz/plantparts.html> to find out which parts of plants we eat.

  - <http://www.naturegrid.org.uk/plant/parts.html#top> and <http://classroom.jc-schools.net/sci-units/food.htm> are sites about parts of plants.

  - <http://www.crickweb.co.uk/ks1science.html> is a very useful site about plants' parts and needs.

Preparation

- Obtain a punnet of flowering plant seedlings (such as petunias) so the pupils can view the roots and root hairs. Later, the petunias (or similar) can be planted in pot plants in a sunny position in the classroom or in a garden bed in the school grounds.

- Pupils will need access to a dictionary or the internet to discuss and answer the final question on page 32.

- Collect the materials listed for the experiment on page 33. It can be carried out in small groups with adult assistance. Magnifying glasses could be supplied to view the cut celery more closely.

The lessons

- Pages 31 and 32 should be used together.

- Carefully remove a seedling from the punnet so pupils can identify each part of a flowering plant while reading and discussing the text on page 31. Flowering plants could also be observed in the school grounds.

- Discuss the answers the pupils wrote to Questions 4 and 5 on page 32.

- The aim of the experiment on page 33 is for the pupils to see how

water travels up through a plant's stem. Celery stalks are ideal as they have a fleshy stem with the xylem (tubes) just visible to the naked eye when a cross-section is cut. A fair test is created by providing a control jar with clear water for the pupils to compare with the jar with liquid containing food colouring. Some time is required to allow the water to work its way up the plant to the leaves of the celery plants.

- After the experiment, discuss how easy or difficult it was to carry out, what worked, what didn't, what changes could be made etc. Lift out the stalk and cut a section to allow the pupils to see the food colouring in the xylem. This is the cross-section of the tubes which carry water up the stalk to the leaves.

Answers

Page 32

1. (c)

2. Teacher check

3. (a) hold the plant in the soil
   (b) water and food to other parts of the plant
   (c) make food for the plant
   (d) part where the seeds are made

4. Answers should indicate they both carry water and food to the leaves and branches and hold up the plant.

5. Answers should indicate that if a plant lost its leaves, the plant would have no way to make food and would die.

The work of scientists question
Nature and development of science
A botanist is a scientist who studies plants so we can learn more about how they help us and their place in the world of living things.

Page 33

1.–3. Teacher check

4. (a) The leaves of the celery gradually turned the colour of the food colouring. The liquid level went down over time.

   (b) The coloured water was gradually absorbed by the stem and travelled up to the leaves. (If the water did not reach the leaves, they would wilt and flop.)

What are the main parts of a plant? – I

Read the text.

A plant is a living thing. Flowers, bushes, trees, grasses and herbs are plants. Most plants grow in the ground.

The different parts of a plant do different things.

The flowers are the part where seeds are made.

The seeds will become new plants.

Different plants have different flowers.

The leaves make food for the plant.

Different plants have different leaf shapes.

Most leaves are green.

Stems act like straws. They carry water and food from the roots to the other parts of the plant.

Stems hold up the leaves and flowers.

There is usually one main stem and smaller side stems.

Trees have a large stem called a trunk, with side stems called branches.

The roots hold the plant in the soil.

The roots have tiny hairs.

They take in water and food from the soil.

What are the main parts of a plant? – 2

Use the text and diagram on page 31 to complete the following.

1. Tick the correct box.

All plants:

(a) grow in the ground. ☐

(b) have flowers. ☐

(c) are living things. ☐

(d) are trees. ☐

2. Draw a line from each label to the correct part of the plant.

flower •

stem •

• leaf

• root

3. Write what each part does.

(a) roots: _____

(b) stems: _____

(c) leaves: _____

(d) flowers: _____

4. How are a tree trunk and a flower's stem alike?

_____

5. What could happen if a plant lost all its leaves?

_____

What is a botanist? What does a botanist do?

The celery experiment

1. You will need:

- 2 clear glass jars or vases
- water
- tablespoon
- marker
- food colouring (red, blue or purple)
- plastic knife
- 2 celery stalks with leaves (cut stalk about 3 cm from base)

2. Follow the steps:

(a) Half fill each container with water. Write 'A' on one and 'B' on the other.

(b) Add 1 tablespoon of food colouring to Container B. Mix.

(c) Place a celery stalk into each container. Leave it for a while.

3. Predict what will happen to the plant and water in:

(a) Container A.

_____

_____

(b) Container B.

_____

_____

4. (a) Write what happened with the celery stalk in Container B.

_____

_____

(b) Write why it happened. _____

_____

_____

Where are living things found?

Content focus:	Different habitats of living things
Investigative skill focus:	Questioning and predicting
	Planning and conducting
	Processing and analysing data and information
	Evaluating
	Communicating

Background information

- A habitat is the native environment or kind of place where a given animal or plant lives or grows. This includes warm seas, mountain tops, fresh waters etc. Simply speaking, a habitat is the place where a population of living organisms exist. A habitat supplies all the needs of the living things, including food, shelter, water, temperature, oxygen, and minerals.

- Pupils can refer to animal habitats in terms of animals homes, such as cave, tree, nest, stable, burrow etc.

- Refer to <http://wwf.panda.org/about_our_earth/ecoregions/about/habitat_types/habitats/> for teacher background information about specific habitats and the animals which live there, and <http://www.bbc.co.uk/schools/ks2bitesize/science/living_things/plants_animals_environment/read1.shtml> for information and games. Additional information about biomes/habitats can also be found at <http://www.enchantedlearning.com/biomes/>.

Preparation

- Young children love learning facts about plants and animals. If possible, read a variety of factual texts about different plants and animals to the pupils before commencing this set of pages. A series of topical books for pupil use in free time is a valuable resource and provides the opportunity for pupils to select books to be read to the class.

- A series of colour pictures showing plants and other living things in different habitats could initiate discussion and guide pupil thinking.

- All the materials to create the worm habitat on page 37 will need to be collected ahead of time. If using plastic drink bottles, the tops will need to be cut off in readiness. Adult helpers may need to be assigned to assist the pupils with the task. The worms should only be collected the day before making the habitat and returned to the earth or compost heap at the conclusion of the experiment.

The lessons

- Read the text with the pupils, making reference to the pictures of the animals which belong to each habitat.

- Pupils should use only the animals and habitats mentioned on page 35 to answer the questions on page 36. They are expected to copy the name labels of the animals to answer Question 1 on page 36.

- Pupils will need to use their general knowledge to answer Question 3. If necessary, discuss each habitat first to enable the pupils to answer the questions easily.

- Some adult assistance may be needed to create the worm habitats using the procedure on page 37.

Answers

Page 36

1. (a) camel   (b) frog
   (c) scorpion   (d) polar bear
2. Teacher check
3. habitats
4. in the water: seaweed, starfish; in a dry place: cactus, lizard
5. Answers will vary slightly but should indicate the following:
   (a) Polar bears have a thick, warm coat of fur to keep them warm.
   (b) Monkeys have hands and arms suitable for climbing trees.
   (c) Frogs have webbed toes to help them swim in water.
   (d) Camels have a fatty hump that provides food and nourishment when food and water is scarce. (It does not contain water.)

Page 37

1.–2. Teacher check
3. (a) The worms should be able to live well in the new habitat as they will have food, and dark, cool conditions.
   (b) The worms will eat the food and tunnel through the layers. They will deposit worm 'castings' to keep the soil moist and healthy.
   (c) As the worms burrow through the jar, they will mix the soil and the sand.
4. Teacher check
- For more information about worms, refer to <http://www.allaboutworms.com/how-do-worms-survive-in-the-soil>.

Where are living things found? – I

Read the text.

Living things are found in many different places.

Living things can be found where it is hot or cold.

camel

polar bear

Living things can be found where it is wet or dry.

frog

scorpion

Living things can be found in trees or in the grass.

monkey

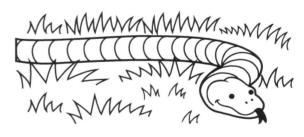

snake

Living things can be found in the water or on dry land.

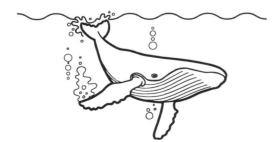

whale

person

Places where living things are found are called **habitats**.

Where are living things found? – 2

Use the text and pictures on page 35 to complete the answers.

1. Copy the name of one animal for each place.

    (a) A hot place

    _____

    (b) A wet place

    _____

    (c) A dry place

    _____

    (d) A cold place

    _____

2. Draw your favourite animal from Question 1.

3. What are places where living things are found called?

    _____

4. Write the names of the living things in the correct habitat.

cactus seaweed starfish lizard	In the water	In a dry place

5. Different living things each have special things that help them survive in their habitat. Write one way each living thing below has done this. Each has a hint to help you.

    (a) polar bear (coat) _____

    (b) monkey (hands/arms) _____

    (c) frog (feet) _____

    (d) camel (hump) _____

Make a worm habitat

1. You will need:

   - clean glass jar (or plastic drink bottle with the top cut off)
   - shoebox with the lid taped (like a hinged door) and holes poked in the end
   - soil
   - sand
   - leaves
   - worms
   - food scraps such as bits of banana skin and lettuce

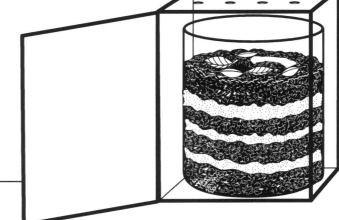

2. Follow the steps:

   (a) Fill jar with layers of soil and sand.

   (b) Place leaves, banana skin and lettuce pieces on top.

   (c) Carefully add the worms to jar.

   (d) Place jar inside the shoebox and tape door shut.

   (e) Place in a cool, dry, dark place outside for a few days.

3. Predict what will happen inside the jar.

   (a) Do you think the worms will be able to live inside the jar?

Yes	No

   Why? _____

   _____

   (b) What do you think the worms will do inside the jar?

   _____

   (c) What do you think will happen to the layers in the jar?

   _____

4. Colour the correct word.

   It was | hard | easy | to make a worm habitat.

What do plants and animals do in different seasons?

Content focus:	Seasonal changes affect plants and animals
Investigative skills focus:	Questioning and predicting
	Planning and conducting
	Processing and analysing data and information
	Communicating

Background information

- The seasons are the result of the Earth's tilted axis. Most places have four seasons—summer, autumn, winter and spring. Each season brings a change in the temperature and weather.

- In some places it is warm all year round, and these places have two seasons—a wet and a dry.

- Plants and animals sense the change in the environment from season to season and are affected by, and adapt to, these changes.

- Plants make their own food using energy from the sun, water, carbon dioxide and a chemical called chlorophyll (which gives plants their green colour). During winter, when daylight hours decrease, there is less light for photosynthesis so the green chlorophyll disappears from the leaves and the leaves change colour. Plants might also lose their leaves or stop growing as an adaptation to cold weather. Plants emerge from this dormant state in spring when more sunlight shines on them.

- Some animals live in habitats that are difficult to survive in all year. They have to find a way to deal with seasonally varying food, shelter and water. As there is less food available for animals in winter, some animals migrate to locations where food is more plentiful; e.g. swallows and swifts. Some animals hibernate in protected places through the winter; e.g. hedgehogs, dormice and bats.

- Long-necked turtles are brown, black or green. They have a long neck and webbed feet with claws to help them walk on land.

- Useful websites:
  - <http://learnenglishkids.britishcouncil.org/en/songs/the-leaves-the-tree> (a song about the leaves of a tree changing in the different seasons)

  - <http://www.saburchill.com/hfns02/chapters/chap011.html> (information about how seasonal changes affect animals and links to hibernation and migration information)

Preparation

- Obtain some pictures (possibly from calendars) of nature scenes in different seasons.

The lessons

- Ensure the children understand what the seasons are and how the weather changes from season to season.

- Read a book such as *The seasons of Arnold's apple tree* by Gail Gibbons. If possible, show the children some pictures of similar trees in different seasons, or nature scenes from calendars of different seasons. Ask the children to describe the scenes and what is the same or different as the seasons change.

- The aim of the activity on page 41 is for the children to create a simple book that demonstrates how the change in seasons affects the life of a long-necked turtle. After reading the story with the children, they colour the turtle (brown, black or green), cut out the pages and staple them in order to make a book. The pages have not been numbered so the children, when putting the pages in order, need to think about the sequence of events and how they follow the sequence of seasons. The children can read or guess the words based on the pictures to help them get the order right.

Answers

Page 40

1. Picture 1 summer (green), picture 2 winter (grey), picture 3 spring (pink), picture 4 autumn (orange)

2. Winter to spring

3. Teacher check

Page 41

Sequence: Cover page, This is a long-necked turtle, In winter she sleeps, In spring she wakes up, In summer she lays eggs, In autumn the babies hatch.

Additional activity

- The children can choose an animal and find out how it gets ready for, or what it does to survive, during winter. They can paint the animal and write a sentence explaining how it gets ready, e.g. 'Hedgehogs sleep in winter'.

What do plants and animals do in different seasons? – I

In **summer**:

Fruits and plants grow.

Insects and animals are very active.

In **autumn**:

Some leaves change colour or fall off the trees.

Some animals grow more hair.

In **winter**:

Some animals sleep all winter.

Some animals move away to a warmer place.

Some plants stop growing.

In **spring**:

New plants, leaves and

flowers grow.

Many animals have babies.

Some animals lose hair.

What do plants and animals do in different seasons? – 2

1.  colour the winter tree GREY   • the spring tree PINK
   • the summer tree GREEN • the autumn tree ORANGE

2. This dog is losing lots of hair.

(Circle) the seasons it is changing from:

     summer to autumn

     winter to spring

3. ✂ cut out and ⬜ glue the animals and plants into the right season.

winter	summer

Long-necked turtle's seasons

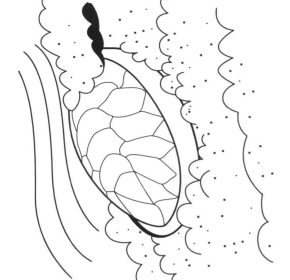

In winter, she sleeps.

In autumn, the babies hatch.

This is a long-necked turtle.

In spring, she wakes up.

Long-necked turtle's seasons

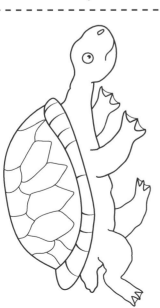

In summer, she lays eggs.

What is it?

The work of scientists: Nature and development of science
Content focus: Humans have five senses
Senses are used to explore and observe

Investigative skills focus: Questioning and predicting
Planning and conducting
Processing and analysing data and information
Communicating

Background information

- Humans and animals have five principal senses, special faculties connected to certain body organs that perceive stimuli and send signals to the brain, where they are interpreted. These senses are hearing, sight, smell, touch and taste. Humans use these senses to gain knowledge of the world and themselves.

- Many scientists believe humans have more than five senses. These additional senses include pain, balance, thirst and hunger.

- The senses often work together. For example, our eyes and nose also help us to taste. You can experiment with this by tasting different jelly beans with your eyes closed and nose blocked.

- Useful website:
  - <http://www.kidcyber.com.au/topics/body_senses.htm> (has information and links to other pages of information about the five senses)

Preparation

- Obtain magazines for children to cut pictures from for Question 2 on page 44.

- Collect popcorn kernels and a popcorn maker for the experiment on page 45.

The lessons

- There are many books, rhymes, songs and fingerplays about the five senses. Try a website such as <http://rhymes.yakaberry.com/5senses.html> for an introductory song or rhyme.

- If possible, take the children outside to a dry grassed area where they can lie down on their backs. Ask them to lie quietly with their eyes closed. Ask them to think about how they know what is around them—how they know this even though they can't see. Ask them to share things they can smell, hear and feel. Discuss how these senses help us to know and explore the world around us. Introduce sight and taste, and discuss how certain body parts help us to find things out.

- The aim of the experiment on page 45 is for the children to use all of their senses in observing popcorn before, during and after popping. Ensure the children, when tasting un-popped popcorn, do not try to chew or swallow it. To avoid accidental swallowing or choking, the children should only lick the kernels with their tongues, and not put them into their mouths. The children can draw how the corn looks and write their other observations or an adult can scribe for them. After the experiment, ask the children to share their observations and compare similarities and differences.

Answers

Page 44

1.–3. Teacher check

Page 45

1.–3. Teacher check

Additional activities

- Place a variety of different textured objects on a display table. The children pick up, feel and describe the objects.

- Put a number of different objects in a box (such as wool, a rock, a rubber band, a seashell, a feather, a piece of ribbon, a toy car, a tennis ball and a spoon). One child at a time puts a hand in the box and tries to guess what he or she is feeling.

- Make sound boxes by putting small objects (such as marbles, rice, paper clips, sand, seeds) into empty boxes, cans or other containers. The children shake and try to identify the objects inside based on the sound they make as the container is moved.

- Read *The gingerbread man*. Make, smell and taste gingerbread men. The children can colour in a drawing of a gingerbread man, then glue ginger (the spice) onto the gingerbread man.

- Find out about animals that have better hearing or smell than people. For example, a dog's nose is much more sensitive than ours, and dogs can hear sounds that humans cannot hear. Dogs can use these senses to help us; for example, police 'sniffer' dogs.

- Discuss the safety issues of things that the children should not touch, such as sharp objects, power points, medicines and flames or hot items.

- Find out how people who have lost one or more of their senses sense the world.

What is it? – I

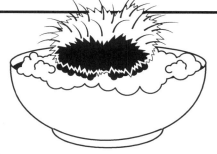

What is this? Is it soft? Is it alive?

How can we find out?

We can find out about things by using our **senses**.

Our **eyes** can **see**.

What colour is it? Is it big or small? Does it move?

Our **hands** can **feel.**

Is it hard or soft?
Is it warm or cold?

Our **nose** can **smell**.

Does it smell nice or bad?

Our **ears** can **hear.**

Is it loud or quiet?

Our **mouth** can **taste**.

Is sweet or salty?

 out finding one of the things from this page.

What is it? – 2

1. 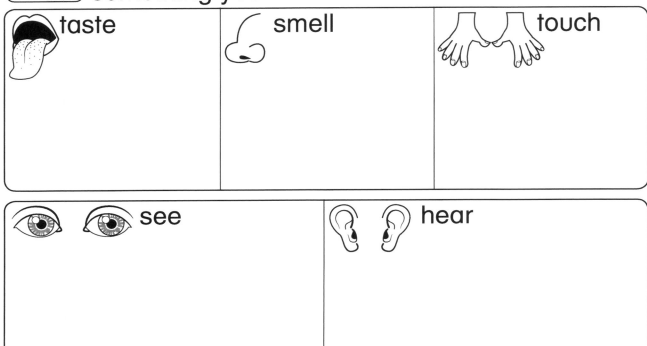 draw something you like to:

taste	smell	touch

see	hear

2. cut and glue a picture of something that is:

red	soft	quiet

3. draw a line to match the body part to the sense.

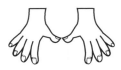

see	hear	touch	smell	taste

Sensational snack!

Materials:

- popcorn kernels • popcorn machine

Steps:

1. 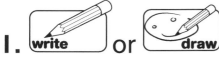 or 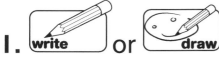 how the un-popped corn:

looks 👁	feels 🖐	smells 👃	tastes 👅

2. Cook the popcorn. Write what you hear.

3. write and draw how the popped corn:

looks 👁	feels 🖐	smells 👃	tastes 👅

How can objects be sorted?

Chemical sciences

The work of scientists:	Nature and development of science
Content focus:	Sorting objects by characteristics
Investigative skills focus:	Questioning and predicting
	Planning and conducting
	Processing and analysing data and information
	Communicating

Background information

- Young children may use the word 'things' to describe objects.

- Young children will need to predominantly use their senses of sight and touch to sort and group different materials. Play games such as selecting an object from a 'feely bag'. The children must feel (without seeing) and state what the object is. They check by looking after guessing.

- Develop vocabulary relating to the sense of touch, such as 'smooth', 'rough', 'bumpy', 'hard', 'soft' etc. Develop vocabulary relating to the sense of sight, including 'large/big', 'small/little', colour words, shape words such as 'triangle', 'circle', 'round', 'rectangle', 'square', 'oval', 'straight', 'crooked', 'light', 'heavy' etc.

- Visit <http://www.crickweb.co.uk/ks1science.html> (an interactive activity about sorting)

Preparation

- Read books such as *We're different; We're the same* (A Sesame Street picture book written by Bobbi Kates and illustrated by Joe Mathieu).

- Play a number of games relating to 'same' and 'different'. Ask children to stand if they have the same eyes, socks, shoes, top, trousers, shorts, dress or length or colour hair etc. Find two children or a group of children with something different. Encourage the children to use the words 'same' and 'different'.

- The children may find, feel and draw pictures of soft and hard objects in the room before completing the activity on page 48.

The lessons

- Pages 46 to 49 should be used together.

- When choosing objects for the children to circle, tick, cross or colour on page 47, describe the object by attributes, colour and use. For example, 'I am thinking of an object in the picture which is small and hard. It is something you can read. What object is it? Circle it'. Capable children may be asked to choose an object and describe it for the others to identify. Extend this activity by asking the children to draw pictures of objects they have in their room at home. An adult may scribe a label for each and, if possible, ask the children to describe each object by its attributes. Directed questions such as, 'Is it big? Is it small? What colour is it? How does it feel?' should be used.

- Read the words 'soft' and 'hard' to the children so they know what groups the cut-out pictures will be sorted into. Assist if necessary.

- Ensure no more than 10 objects are used for each type of material on page 49. Before sorting the objects, ask the children which ones they think there will be more of or less of. Will they fit in the muffin cups? After the sorting activity, ask questions such as 'Was it easy or hard to sort the materials?', 'Did you enjoy the activity? Why or why not?', 'What other objects could be sorted using the muffin tins?'

Answers

Page 48

- soft objects: teddy bear, pillow, pyjamas; hard objects: book, toy car, crayon, puzzle piece, bed

Page 49

Teacher check

Additional activities

- Sort large geometric shapes by colour, size and thickness.

- Rub over rough surfaces using a crayon and sheet of paper to make pictures of their textures.

- Compare playdough that has been allowed to go hard to one kept in a container with an airtight lid.

- Cut out pictures from coloured magazines which are all the same colour. Glue them onto a large sheet of paper.

- Use a variety of materials with different textures, colours, shapes and sizes to create a collage picture of a particular object.

- Have the children sort leftover pieces of broken wax crayons into muffin containers and heat in a oven heated to about 120 °C for about 20 minutes. Show the children how the hard crayons became soft and melted partway through baking. They will melt into easy-to-handle large pieces. Cool well before allowing the children to use them. NOTE: The children should pull off all the paper wrapping from the crayons before baking.

- Encourage the children to keep the collage trolley and recycled materials boxes tidy by sorting them.

- Ask the children to compare two objects by hefting (lifting by hand) to find out which is heavy and which is light.

How can objects be sorted? – I

There are objects all around us.

We can **see** them.

We can **feel** them.

Some **look** and **feel** the same.

Some **look** and **feel** different.

Instructions: Read the text to the children. Ask the children what objects they see in the picture. Select specific objects for them to circle, tick or cross.

How can objects be sorted? – 2

1.  out the pictures of the objects.

2.  the pictures in the correct box.

soft

hard

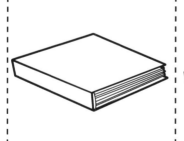   

 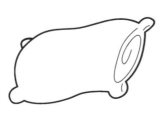 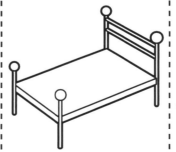 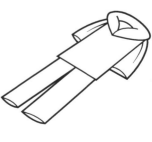

Sorting objects

Sort dry materials into groups.

Results:

1.  and each material.

2.  the number of each.

Instructions: Materials: 12-case muffin tin; dried peas, lentils, beans, pumpkin or sunflower seeds; dry macaroni; clean hands; mixing bowl or flat baking tray
Steps: 1. Mix some of each dried material into bowl or tray. 2. Sort materials into muffin cases.

What can it do?

Chemical sciences

The work of scientists:	Nature and development of science
Content focus:	Materials have different properties which make them useful for creating objects
Investigative skills focus:	Questioning and predicting
	Planning and conducting
	Processing and analysing data and information
	Communicating

Background information

- Materials are made from matter. This can be anything from wood, cement, water, air, metal, cotton, glass to plastic.

- Refer to <http://www.woodlands-junior.kent.sch.uk/revision/Science/changingmaterials.htm> (a variety of resources relating to the topic)

Preparation

- Books may be a helpful aid in introducing the topic or consolidating concepts after completing this set of pages. Some examples include: Acorn books science series by Charlotte Guillain (*Smooth or rough/ Stiff or bendy/Shiny or dull/Heavy or light/Hard or soft*), Little Science stars: *What things are made of* by Helen Orme, *Materials: Plastic/Glass/Metal/Rubber/Wood* by Cassie Mayer.

- Collect examples of materials from the text on page 51 to show to the children.

The lessons

- Show, and allow the children to feel and lift, examples of the materials in the text on page 51. Discuss what they feel like and where the children may have seen objects made from them. Some children may suggest that some of the objects are soft and bendy, strong and smooth etc.

- Read and discuss page 51 with the children. Ask for other suggestions for types of materials and objects made from them.

- On page 52, the children are matching objects to materials they would most likely be made from. After they have completed the page, ask questions about other materials the same objects *could be* made from. 'Would bricks make a good pillow? Why or why not?' (Responses might include: because they would be too hard/ they would hurt your head when you lie on them etc.) 'What other materials would be good for making a house?' (Responses may include: wood or steel because they are strong). If time allows, the children could bend pipe-cleaners into flower shapes to be placed later into a small pot or empty vase.

- On page 53, the children must find (or draw) pictures of objects made from strong, soft, see-through (transparent), shiny or smooth material or materials which can float. Discuss what type of objects are strong, shiny, smooth, soft, see-through (transparent) or can float. Emphasise that these must be objects and not animals.

Answers

Page 52

- house—bricks, pillow—feathers, sweater—wool, bridge—steel, craft flowers—pipe cleaners NOTE: Some children may suggest that a house can be made from steel and a bridge from bricks. Accept these answers, but state that according to the picture, the answers are as above.

Page 53

- Suggested pictures for the children to look for: strong—house, cricket bat, rope etc; soft—pyjamas, hair, ice-cream etc; see-through—windows, cling film plastic, glass, clear plastic etc; shiny—mirror, saucepan, tinsel, Christmas decorations, lights, CD etc; float—boat, raft, cork, life jacket, arm bands, light objects such as a sheet of paper, big plastic ball etc; smooth—rock washed smooth by water, vase, bottle, apple etc.

Additional activities

- Ask the children to build strong structures such as bridges, houses, roads etc. using rigid materials like wooden blocks. Children should tell how they made their structure and why they used particular shapes and sizes of blocks.

- Allow free use of a variety of building materials, including Lego™ blocks, connectable plastic sticks, playdough or clay, cardboard strips etc.

- Use printing techniques such as the side of a cardboard strip to create the appearance of wood or bricks on a craft house shape.

- Look at, feel and list different types of materials used in the classroom or at home. These could include glass, wood, plastic, brick, granite, laminex™, aluminium etc. Use large charts and add cut-out pictures of objects made from these materials.

- Compile a feeling chart for the children. Label sections 'soft', 'hard', 'rough', 'smooth' etc. and attach light objects for each label for the children to feel. View some ideas at <http://www.flickr.com/groups/classrmdisplays/pool/tags/classroomdisplays/page7/>.

- Collect different types of natural objects, such as bark, pine cones, leaves, flowers or rocks, from the playground. In the classroom, sort these into groups.

What can it do? – I

Materials are different.

Some materials can **bend**.

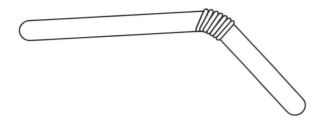 

Some materials can **stretch**.

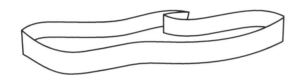 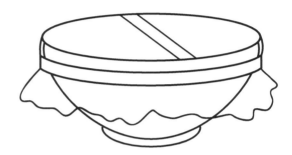

Some materials are **strong**.

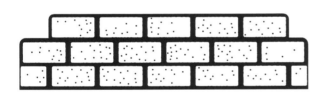 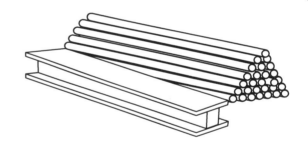

Some materials are **soft**.

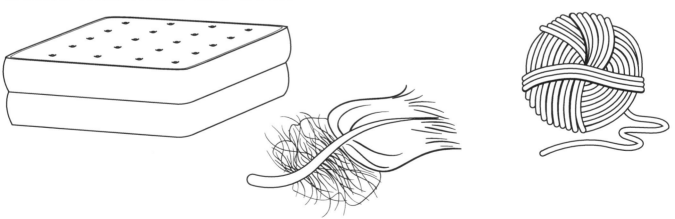

Different materials can do different things.

This makes them good for making different objects.

What can it do? – 2

 draw a line to match the object to the best material.

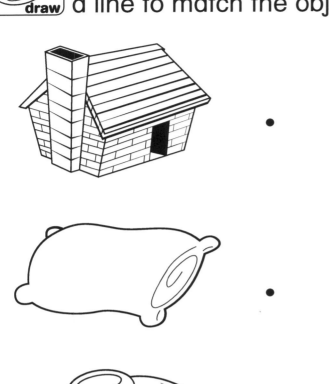

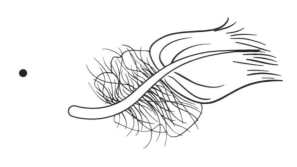

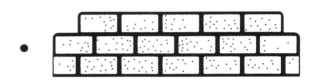

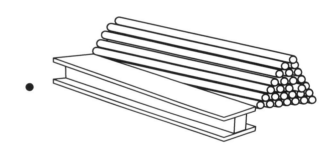

Objects and materials table

✂ cut out and 🖌 glue pictures of objects made from each type of material.

strong	soft
see through	**shiny**
float	**smooth**

What is this building made from?

The work of scientists:	Nature and development of science
Content focus:	Types of shelters and buildings and materials they are made from
Investigative skills focus:	Questioning and predicting
	Planning and conducting
	Processing and analysing data and information
	Communicating

Background information

- Young children need to become aware that materials have a purpose. They are used to make objects. The type of objects they are used for depends on the type of material and how it acts or what it can do.

- Songs about building and construction can be found at <http://www.ccplonline.org/kids/songs4tots.html>. Visit <http://www.youtube.com/watch?v=3_tR59hcxwo> to view a video of the story of *This is the house that Jack built*.

Preparation

- Ensure the pupils have access to red, grey, green, yellow, blue and other coloured pencils or crayons to complete page 55.

- Find a copy of *The three little pigs* to read to the children before completing page 56.

The lessons

- Read the story *This is the house that Jack built*. (Or watch the clip mentioned above). Talk about what Jack built the house from. Read and talk about page 55 with the children. Follow the teacher's instructions as shown at the side of the page. The page may be cut up and glued onto individual pages and a sentence scribed about each. Keep the work when completed as a reminder for the following lesson or enlarge a copy to A3 size as a reminder for the lesson on page 56.

- Review the enlarged version of page 55 and state what each house is made from. On page 56, look at the word pictures of bricks, glass, stone, grass, canvas and ice then as a group discuss and circle the word 'strong', 'light' or both for each material. Read the sentence about the three little pigs and the words at the bottom of the page. The children cut out the words and glue each under the correct house.

- Read the story of the gingerbread man to the children. Talk about what a real gingerbread house is made from and what it looks like. Ask 'Would gingerbread be a good material to build a real house from? Why/Why not?' Ask what would happen if the gingerbread was left out in the rain like a real house. When the children have finished gluing on materials such as matchsticks to their gingerbread house, ask them to say whether they like their house, whether they think it looks good, what other materials they could have used etc. They might like to compare their finished products.

Answers

Pages 55–57

Teacher check

Additional activities

- Provide some large plastic tubs. Label with the words 'plastic', 'wood' and 'metal'. Ask the children to place small objects made from each material in the tubs as well as drawings or cut-out pictures of objects made from each in the same tubs.

- The children sort familiar objects into two different groups, such as 'see-through' (transparent) and 'not see-through' (opaque), 'thick' and 'thin', 'strong' and 'weak', 'bendy/stretchy' (flexible) and 'not bendy/stretchy (rigid) or 'rough' and 'smooth'. Select an object from each group and ask 'Would this object be good to make a — from? Why/Why not?'

- Provide large examples of waterproof material, such as rubber and non-waterproof fabric, such as woollen material. Use a miniature watering can to test which ones are suitable for making a raincoat. Ask the children to say why/why not.

- Hold a material hunt in the room searching for objects made from plastic, metal, wood, clay/pottery or cardboard. Describe and discuss the objects.

- Play 'What am I?' games. The children listen to clues about an object in the classroom, including what it is made from and guess what it is.

- In the dress-up corner, place a plastic hard hat and tool set and wood for the children to 'build' shelters and buildings.

- List the names of, and draw pictures of the shelters of, different animals. For example, stable—horse, kennel—dog etc. Talk about what materials they could be made from and why.

- As a class activity, with adult assistance, mix, cook and build a gingerbread house. The children may assist by adding sweets to decorate the house. Discuss which sweets would be suitable or resemble real building materials. Eat when completed.

What is this building made from? – 1

✔ the one that looks most like your house.

Prim-Ed Publishing®   www.prim-ed.com

SCIENCE – Book 1

What is this building made from? – 2

1. (Circle) the correct word.

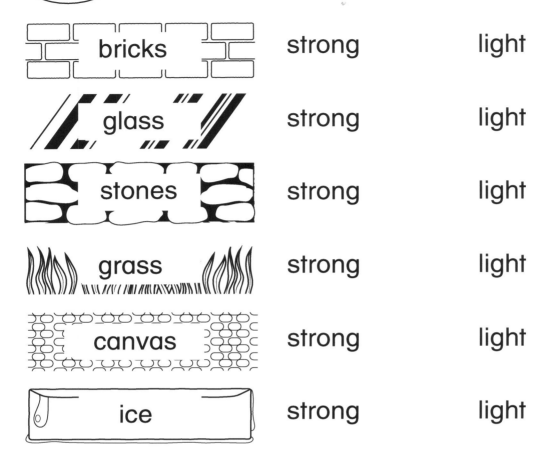

	strong	light
bricks	strong	light
glass	strong	light
stones	strong	light
grass	strong	light
canvas	strong	light
ice	strong	light

The three little pigs have forgotten what their homes are made from.

2. ✂ cut and 🖊 glue the words to match each building.

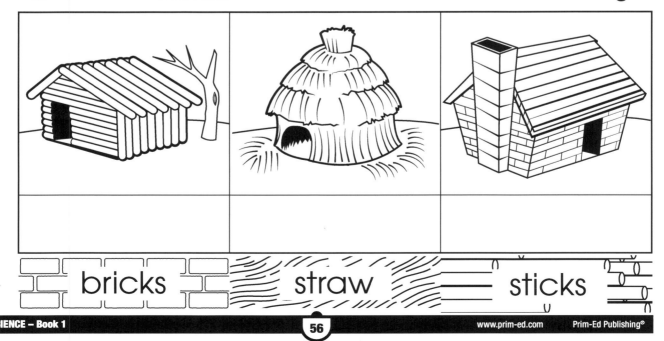

bricks   straw   sticks

Chemical sciences

Gingerbread house

Trace the word that tells what this house is made from.

g i n g e r b r e a d

What are these clothes good for?

Chemical sciences

Content focus:	Different types of clothing for different purposes
Investigative skills focus:	Questioning and predicting
	Planning and conducting
	Processing and analysing data and information
	Communicating

Background information

- There are four main factors which influence the wearing of particular types of clothing—fashion, feel, fit and function.

- Comfort is perhaps the primary purpose of clothing. In hot climates, people wear clothing to protect them from hot sun and winds, and keep them cool. In cold climates, clothing provides insulation from cold winds and low temperatures.

- The seasons affect the type of clothing worn—thinner, lighter, loose (and less) clothing is worn in warmer seasons; while heavier, thicker, and many layers of clothing are worn in colder seasons.

- Clothing also provides protection from hazards such as weather, injury, chemicals, insects etc.

- Stories such as *Puss in boots*, *The emperor's new clothes*, *Little Red Riding Hood* and *Cinderella* (from rags to a beautiful ball gown) would be useful resources to support this set of pages about clothing. Versions of these stories may be found at< http://www.popularchildrenstories.com/stories.htm >.

- Find songs about clothing at <http://www.preschooleducation.com/sclothes.shtml>. The website <http://songsforteaching.com/calendarweatherseasons/whatevertheweatherjackiesilberg.htm> has songs called 'Whatever the weather' and 'What else do I need', which support this set of pages.

Preparation

- Collect shopping catalogues which show children's clothing.

- If possible, collect and display examples of the clothing when completing page 60.

- Collect and cut up small pieces of material such as waterproof plastic, cotton material, fleecy material etc. for the activity on page 61.

The lessons

- View the catalogues and discuss the suitability of different clothing for different purposes. For example, 'Would you wear the pyjamas in this picture to go to the cinema?' etc. Sing songs such as 'This is the way we put on our raincoat ... On a rainy day'. Make up verses which relate to the pictures on page 59. Read the sentences with the children, and ask them to cut out the pieces and then staple them together to make a simple take-home book.

- Question 1 on page 60 asks the children to match clothing worn when undertaking specific activities. Discuss other activities such as boating, which requires a life jacket, or playing on the beach in a hot country, which will require protective clothing such as a rash guard shirt or suit. Identify articles of clothing which are for protection or safety, such as the helmet needed to ride a bike.

- Enlarge the worksheet on page 61 to A3 size to enable the children to glue on larger pieces of a variety of materials. These may all be red to make the cape look more effective. Discuss the types of material cut up and what each may be good for and why. Before the children glue on the selected material, have them evaluate whether the material would make a good cape and why. Help the children relate the materials to clothing they have at home made from similar materials and what they do when they are wearing the clothing. Have the children think up questions to ask Little Red Riding Hood about her clothes.

Answers

Pages 59–61

Teacher check

Additional activities

- Collect a variety of clothing such as a warm coat, T-shirt, pair of sandals and a swimming costume. Ask the children to select the one that does not belong and why. Repeat with other categories, including winter clothes, protective clothing, waterproof clothing or different types of shoes such as boots, party shoes, running shoes, sandals, dress-up high heeled shoes etc.

- Look at pictures of, or examine real clothing, such as a sari, kimono, traditional Chinese suits, grass hula skirts, Greek costumes etc. View some images at < http://www.tsl.state.tx.us/ld/projects/trc/2009/manual/celebrations_libraries.html >. Display dolls in traditional costumes and let the children feel the materials, or make large cardboard or paper dolls with tab clothing for the children to dress. Large dolls in the play corner may be wrapped in pieces of different material to represent various types of clothing.

- Dress-up clothing relating to the stories mentioned in the background information would be useful in the play corner. Other types of clothing such as raincoats and hats, sun hats, knee pads, helmets, hard hats, ball gowns and sparkly shoes etc. may also be included.

SCIENCE – Book 1 58 www.prim-ed.com Prim-Ed Publishing®

What are these clothes good for? – I

Raincoats keep us **dry**.

Sun hats keep us **cool**.

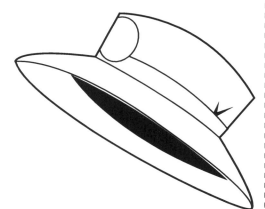

Jumpers keep us **warm**.

Some clothes keep us **safe**.

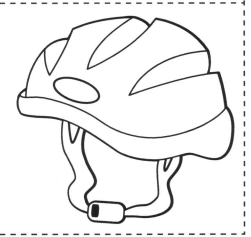

What are these clothes good for? – 2

1. Match the clothes to the activity.

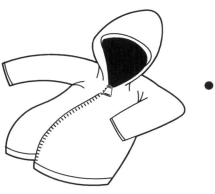

2.  the clothes needed for the activity.

Little Red Riding Hood

 out and glue different materials onto the cape.

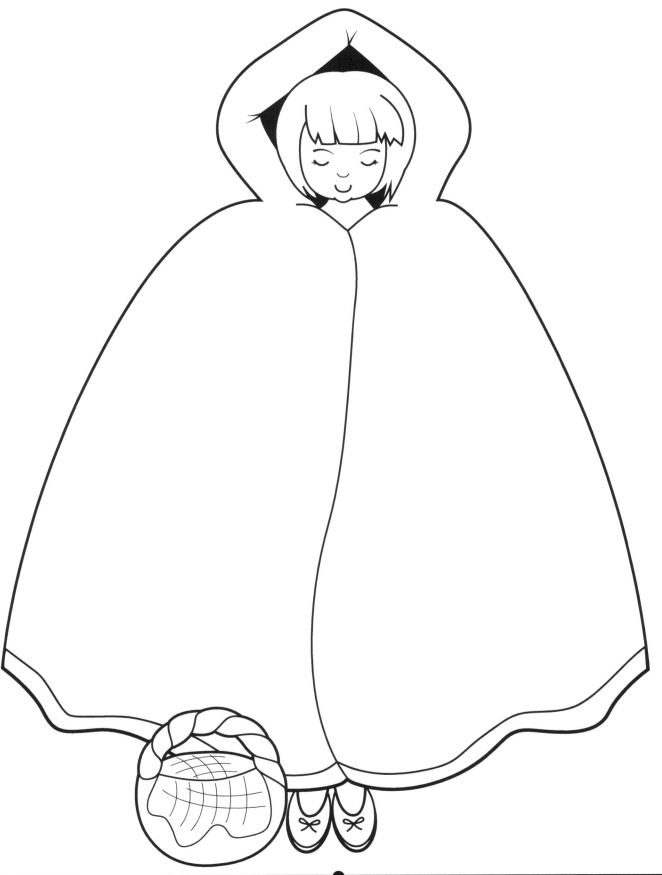

How does it move?

Physical sciences

Content focus:	Objects move in different ways; objects have different shapes; objects move in different ways depending on their shape
Investigative skills focus:	Questioning and predicting
	Planning and conducting
	Processing and analysing data and information
	Communicating

Background information

• This set of pages introduces motion and simple forces.

• A force is an influence which produces motion or change of motion of an object. A force can be things such as a push, pull or twist etc.

• Forces can be big, such as the pull of a star on a planet, or very small, such as the pull of a nucleus on an electron. Forces act everywhere in the universe at all times.

• Visit <http://www.bbc.co.uk/schools/scienceclips/ages/5_6/pushes_pulls.shtml> (games for children about pushes and pulls)

Preparation

• Collect examples of toys which move in different ways, such as a hula hoop, toy sailboat, pinwheel, kite, ball etc. Include those depicted on pages 63 – 65 as well as the other objects shown.

• Ensure the children are familiar with the basic shapes—circles, squares, rectangles, triangles and ovals.

• Read the story *And everyone shouted 'Pull!'* or *Push it! Pull it! (A first look at forces and motion)*, both by Claire Llewellyn.

• Read other stories to the children, such as *The enormous turnip*.

The lessons

• After playing with or viewing the collected toys, discuss each picture on page 63. Find out which children have used or seen those shown. Ask how they make them move. Read the words and complete the sentences orally. The children then cut out the pieces, which are stapled together to form a small book with pages that flip up. Encourage the children to try to 'read' the sentences with assistance, using the picture clues.

• The first part of page 64 requires the children to identify the shapes of common objects they see at school, home and in the community. The second part requires them to carry out a simple experiment using the objects in the table to see if they will roll or not. Before testing each object, the children are required to guess (or predict) whether the object will roll or not. The experiment may be completed as a whole class or in small groups with adult assistance.

• Page 65 requires the children to tick the boxes next to pictures of objects to tell which types of forces are needed to make them move. Ask the children 'If you push a block, will it move?' etc. Ideally, use similar actual objects to test before the children tick the boxes. Some objects will have ticks in more than one box.

Answers

Page 63

Teacher check

Page 64

1. The circular objects are: the ball, the empty toilet roll, the wheel/tyre and the tape. The rectangular objects are: the blocks, box of pencils, book and jigsaw puzzle in its base.

2. Teacher check guesses. The empty toilet roll and tape should roll; the box of pencils and the book should not roll.

Page 65

	push	pull	blow	hit
block	✔	✔	✘	✔
ball	✔	✔	✘	✔
teddy bear	✔	✔	✘	✔
pull-along duck	✔	✔	✘	✔
car	✔	✔	✘	✔
rolling cylinder	✔	✔	✘	✔

Additional activities

• In large hoops, sort and place objects by shape—circular (or round), square, rectangular, oval etc.

• In the playground, search for dandelions. Pick them and use a blowing force to make the seeds move (fly).

• With adult assistance, the children make and blow a pinwheel or paper sailboat to make it move.

• The children slide down a slippery dip on their backs and stomachs.

• Put objects at the top of a ramp made using a plank of wood with one end resting on the seat of a chair. Let them slide down to see which ones slides the best, quickest or slowest (or not at all).

How does it move? – I

Teacher instructions: The children cut out the pieces. The teacher staples the ten small sheets on top of each other on the right-hand side of the full base sheet. The children flip up the pages to read them with the teacher. Enlarge to A3 size.

Objects move when they …

are pushed.

are pulled.

are rolled.

are blown.

slide.

fly.

spin.

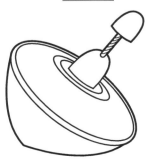

turn.

Physical sciences

How does it move? – 2

1. 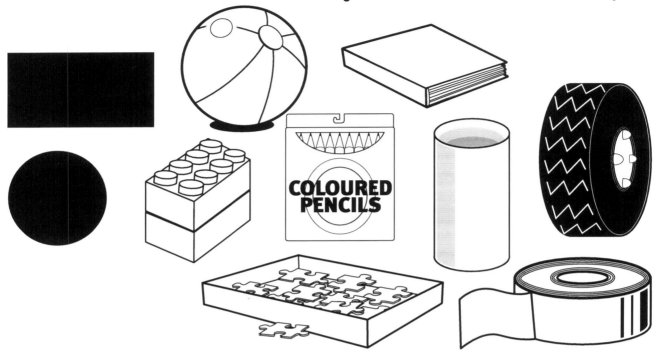 draw a line to match the objects to the correct shape.

2. ✔ the objects that will roll. ✖ the ones that will not.
   Guess first then check. ✔ your guess if it was correct.

Object	Guess	Check

Objects and how they move

✔ the box that tells how it can be moved.

	push	pull	blow	hit

Can balls move differently?

Content focus:	Round objects such as balls roll and bounce well; some bounce higher or better than others
Investigative skills focus:	Questioning and predicting
	Planning and conducting
	Processing and analysing data and information
	Evaluating
	Communicating

Background information

- Galileo Galilei was a famous Italian scientist who is reported to have dropped two different weights from the Leaning Tower of Pisa, showing that they landed at the same time. He also conducted experiments about objects in motion. He used an inclined board with a groove cut into the centre of it to roll brass balls down. He timed their descent using a water clock and compared the time to the distance travelled. He concluded that the distance travelled is proportional to the square of the time. If the distance was doubled, the ball would travel four times as fast. This was because the ball was being constantly accelerated by gravity.

Preparation

- Read stories such as *Three bouncing balls* (Scholastic) or *Stop that ball* by Mike McClintock, to introduce the topic.

- In the playground, hold bouncing ball races over a short distance, with the children being the bouncing balls.

- Let the children feel and bounce real balls of different sizes and shapes. Some examples of different balls may be obtained from the sports storeroom at the school.

The lessons

- On page 67, the children are familiarising themselves with different types of balls as well as learning that balls are round and round things roll well. Some children may only be familiar with a few of them.

- Page 68 involves an experiment. Teachers will need to obtain a long skipping rope (or similar item) to mark the starting position, balls of different weights and sizes, simple flag markers (made by inserting a bamboo skewer through a triangle of coloured cardboard), and a flat area to roll the balls. Lay the skipping rope on the ground to mark the starting point. Choose two children to stand behind the rope. Select two balls of very different weights and sizes such as those on the worksheet. Each child will roll a ball. Have the children stand behind the rope and roll their ball as hard as they can. Then mark where each ball comes to rest with a flag marker. Record on the worksheet by drawing. The children may use a book or hard sheet of cardboard to rest their worksheet on while drawing answers. Alternatively, the sheet may be enlarged and completed as a class. Inside, the children can complete the 'Extra' activities. Have the children talk about the activity. Was it fun? Easy? Hard?

- Before commencing the activity on page 69, have the children look at the different balls and predict (guess) which one will bounce the highest. Check predictions after the activity. To complete the activity, a ruler or growth chart will need to be taped to a wall near a smooth floor. Select a child to bounce each ball as hard as possible. (Demonstrate first.) An adult will need to use a marker to indicate how high each ball bounces on the ruler or growth chart. This number will be the one that the children copy and write on their recording sheet. If possible, simplify the numbers by having large distances between 1 and 10, rather than actual centimetre heights. Later, these results could be recorded on a simple pictogram. Have the children talk about the activity. Was it fun? Easy? Hard?

- Discuss other activities which could be carried out using the balls. Balls may be sorted and placed in order of size, how fast or slow each travels, the bounciest, heaviest etc.

Answers

Pages 67–69

Teacher check

Additional activities

- Select a particular type of ball (such as a heavy cricket ball). Find a length of wood to use as a ramp (inclined plane). If possible, use woodwork glue to glue two lengths of rope or strong twine down the wood to create guides for the ball to travel down without rolling off the ramp. Roll the ball down the ramp, varying the heights of the ramp. As a class, make conclusions such as 'The higher the ramp, the quicker the ball runs down'. Repeat using other balls, and if desired carry out ball races to see which type of ball rolls fastest or slowest down the ramp.

- Using different types of balls, and throwing them down as hard as possible, count the number of bounces each ball does. Which ball bounces the most? Predict (guess) first before doing the activity then check predictions. Were the predictions correct?

- Play familiar games such as 'Catch' using different balls. Then decide which balls were the easiest to use and why.

- Label large coloured pictures of different balls with words such as 'fast', 'slow', 'light', 'heavy' etc.

Can balls move differently? – 1

Round objects roll well. Balls are round.

There are many different types of balls.

1. ✔ the balls you know.

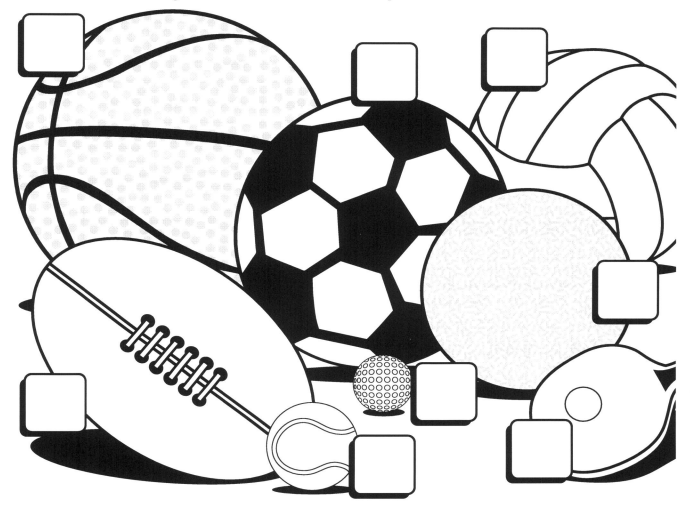

2. draw your favourite type of ball.

3. colour it your favourite colour.

Can balls move differently? – 2

Roll two balls of different weights or sizes.

Results:

 the ball that rolled further.

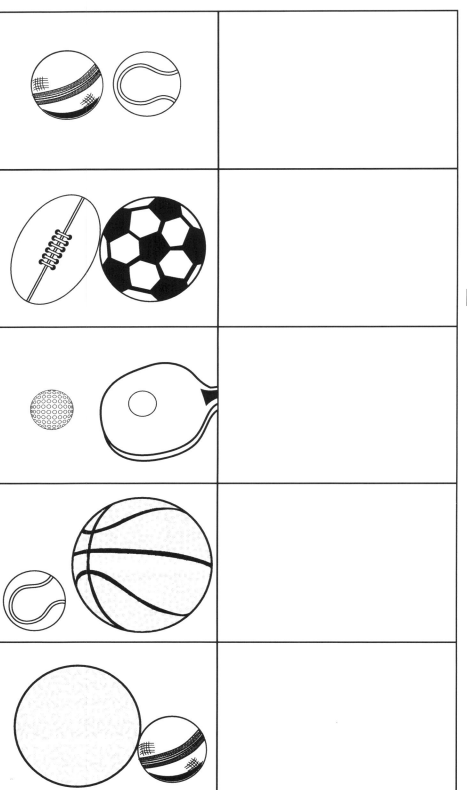

Extra:

- Colour the heavier ball in each pair.

- Tick the bigger ball in each pair or write 'same' if they are the same size.

- Circle the pair of balls that have two different shapes.

Physical sciences

Bouncing balls

1. Drop a ball from a given height.

2. write a number to tell how high it bounced.

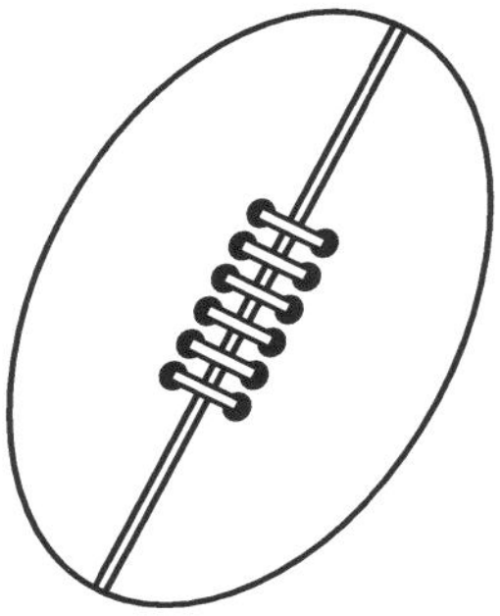

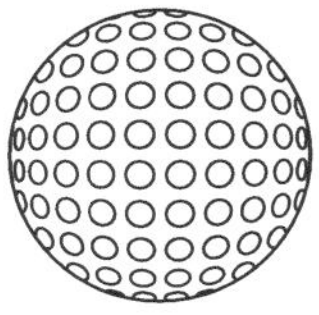

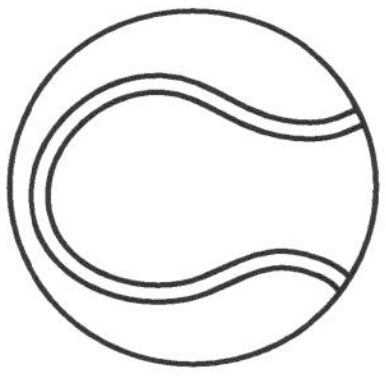

6 —

5 —

4 —

3 —

2 —

1 —

Physical sciences

How can people move?

<table>
<tr><td>**Content focus:**</td><td>People move in many different ways; the ways people move depend on their shape and size and what activity they are doing</td></tr>
<tr><td>**Investigative skills focus:**</td><td>Questioning and predicting</td></tr>
<tr><td></td><td>Planning and conducting</td></tr>
<tr><td></td><td>Processing and analysing data and information</td></tr>
<tr><td></td><td>Communicating</td></tr>
</table>

Background information

- This set of pages relates to movement as a physical science rather than human movement as a part of biological sciences. The words 'push' and 'pull' and 'energy' have been used to explain how arms and legs move, and how people move along the ground or in the water.

- Human beings are mammals who walk upright on two legs (bipeds). Like many other mammals, humans can move in a number of different ways. Humans can run, walk, skip, jump, hop, crawl and imitate the movements of other mammals.

- This set of four pages should be supported by many activities involving different types of movement.

Preparation

- Read the story *From head to toe* by Eric Carle and get the children to perform the animal movements with their own bodies.

- If possible, use a growth chart to continually track the height of the children. Make comparisons such as 'Luke is the tallest person in the class', 'Janet is the smallest person in the class', 'Jack is taller than Bill' etc. This will make the children aware of size and shape. Height and length of legs is used in this set of pages as opposed to 'fat' or 'large' to ensure sensitivity to the children's self-image.

The lessons

- Read and explain each group of sentences on page 71. Look at the pictures and complete the following after the relevant sections: (1) discuss the different shapes and sizes of children; (2) discuss the types of nutritious food children need to move and be healthy; (3) select a child to show how he/she walks by moving his/her arms and legs in slow motion, while the others observe and imitate; (4) have the children walk, skip, jump and hop. Discuss other ways people can move such as crawling, swimming or galloping. Then ask the children to demonstrate how to crawl and gallop.

- Assist the children to complete the activity on page 72. They must cut out the words at the bottom of the page and paste them to complete sentences about themselves and a friend. Each pair of words is also repeated at the end of each sentence so the children know which pair of words they are to choose from. Have the children compare worksheets and 'read' or repeat the sentences to a friend to see the similarities and differences. Accept all answers. Some children may feel they are big compared to a baby brother or sister, or because they are growing up, or old enough to go to school. The important aspect is for the children to realise that some children are the same, some are different and they may move in the same or completely different ways. After completion, ask the children how easy or hard the activity was. This type of simple evaluation should be repeated often to develop the children's skills.

- Page 73 involves the children finding four different people in the classroom—different in stature and the ways they move. After completion, ask the children how easy or hard the activity was. If there is a child in the class who everyone knows is a very fast runner, the children may be asked to predict if that person will be chosen by class members.

Answers

Pages 71–73

Teacher check

Additional activities

- Play games with the children. Have them run as fast as they can in a straight line while you count to ten. Have each child place a marker to indicate the spot where he/she finished. Repeat by having the children jog as slowly as they can for the same time frame. Mark the spot again and compare the difference. Make conclusions, such as, 'When I run fast, I get further than when I jog slowly'.

- Play big steps and little steps. Have the children repeat the timed activity above using 'dolly steps' (heel to toe small steps) and giant steps, then compare the distance again. Repeat using small upright jumps and long, low jumps etc.

- Use a whistle to direct different movements in a given area of the playground. On the word 'Go!', the children begin to run around and when the whistle blows, change their movement to jumping/hopping/skipping or such as directed by the teacher.

- Ask the children to use coloured geometric shapes to create images of themselves. They should think about the shape of their body, legs, head etc.

How can people move? – 1

People are different shapes and sizes.

People need energy to move.

People get energy from the food they eat.

People need to push or pull with their legs or arms to move.

People can run, walk, skip, jump or hop.

People can move fast or slowly.

How can people move? – 2

I.  about yourself.

 out and  words from the bottom.

I am [_____].   **big**   **small**

I run [_____].   **fast**   **slowly**

2.  about a friend.

 out and  words from the bottom.

My friend is [_____].   **big**   **small**

My friend runs [_____].   **fast**   **slowly**

3. Some people are the same.

4. Some people are different.

big	small	fast	slowly
big	small	fast	slowly

SCIENCE – Book 1   72   www.prim-ed.com   Prim-Ed Publishing®

Physical sciences

Different people

Find and [draw] a person in your class.

a big person who runs fast	
a big person who runs slowly	
a little person who runs fast	
a little person who runs slowly	

Physical sciences

How do animals move?

<table>
<tr><td>Content focus:</td><td>Animals are different sizes and shapes; animals move in different ways; the way animals move depends on their size and shape</td></tr>
<tr><td>Investigative skills focus:</td><td>Questioning and predicting</td></tr>
<tr><td></td><td>Planning and conducting</td></tr>
<tr><td></td><td>Processing and analysing data and information</td></tr>
<tr><td></td><td>Communicating</td></tr>
</table>

Background information

- This set of pages relates to movement as a physical science rather than animal movement as a part of biological sciences.

- The ability of animals to move from one location to another is called locomotion. Animal movements are dependent on their habitat, how they need to obtain food or reproduce, and how they protect themselves. To move, animals need energy to overcome friction, drag, inertia and gravity. An animal at rest must push something backwards in order to move forwards—land animals push the ground; swimming animals push water; and flying animals push against the air.

- Animals such as snakes or earthworms move by changing the shape of their bodies to get across the ground or through soil or water.

- Visit <http://www.teachersdomain.org/resource/tdc02.sci.life.colt. move/> (a short video showing how different animals move)

- Visit <http://www.ngsp.com/Resources/ TeacherResourceDownloads/LanguageLiteracyVocabularyWOL/ tabid/65/Default.aspx> (a unit of work about how animals move)

Preparation

- Read stories such as *Pretend you're a cat* by Jean Marzollo and Jerry Pinkney and do actions to verses of familiar songs, such as, 'This is the way we crawl like a ...', 'This is the way we fly like a bat ...' etc.

The lessons

- Enlarge page 75 to A3 size. View instructions for making the book at <http://library.thinkquest.org/J001156/makingbooks/minibook/ index.htm> (Steps 1 to 4 have been eliminated as these are given on the worksheet as cutting and folding lines.) Read and discuss the concepts on the pages. Ask the children to give examples of other animals for each page. The children should role-play the actions of the animals mentioned on each page. The children should state the manner in which each animal depicted moves.

- Page 76 involves classifying animals by their movement. Most of the classifications have details to identify specific animals. Three animals have been chosen for each of the six categories. The children may place the horse in the category of animals that have strong legs and run. This is acceptable as long as they can justify their choice. The headings of the boxes may be written on six large sheets of cardboard for the children to draw or cut out pictures of animals for each category. For best results, enlarge to A3 size. Before the children view the pictures of the animals at the bottom of the page, tell them the categories and have the children guess (predict) which pictures may be on the worksheet for them to cut and paste into each category.

- Enlarge page 77 to A3 size and photocopy onto cardboard. Follow instructions on worksheet. Read *Cows can't fly* by David Milligan.

Answers

Pages 75–77

Teacher check

Additional activities

- Play 'Duck, duck, goose ...' using other animals. For example, 'Bat, bat, bird', 'Fish, fish, dolphin'. These can be the names of animals who all move in the same manner, or the names of two animals that move in the same way and one animal that moves differently; for example, 'Snake, snake, horse'. Ask the children to help select the animal names.

- Sort animals by habitats—air, land or water. Ask: 'Does habitat decide how an animal moves?' For example, 'Can an animal who lives in the water move around by running or digging?'

- Look at many different pictures or photographs of animals moving and ask the children to give a 'doing' word (verb) such as fly, jump, etc. which tells how the animal is moving.

- Select children to role-play the movements of different animals for the other children to guess the animal.

- Give each child a coloured feather from a collection to dance or 'fly' with. Put on some 'airy' music and ask the children to keep their feather 'flying' in the air by blowing.

- Make craft animals that move—birds that flap their wings and fly, fan-folded worms and caterpillars that wiggle, and other animals joined using split pins. Attach string to some so the children have to provide the energy to make them move.

- Teach the children the poem *Jump or jiggle* by Evelyn Beyer.

Physical sciences

How do animals move? – I

1 Many types of animals

2 Animals have different shapes and sizes.

3 Animals need energy to move.

4 Animals get energy to move from the food they eat.

5 Animals can move fast or slowly.

6 Animals can run, walk, jump, hop, swim, crawl, fly and climb.

7 The legs and feet of animals help them move.

8 Animals can move on two legs, four legs or one leg.

Physical sciences

How do animals move? – 2

 out and the pictures in the correct boxes.

Animals with big feet and strong legs that hop.	Animals with webbed feet, fins and flippers that swim.
Animals with strong legs that run.	Animals that have many feet or use their bodies to crawl.
Animals that have wings and fly.	Animals that walk, run and jump.

Physical sciences

Make a moving animal

  out and join with a split pin.

Teacher instructions: The children colour and cut out the pieces. The teacher or an adult helper punches a hole in the body and circular legs indicated by the cross. Join circular legs to body at holes with a split pin. Turn circle to make legs move backwards or forwards. If desired, attach a firm strip of cardboard to the body as a handle so the child has to provide the energy to make the cow move.

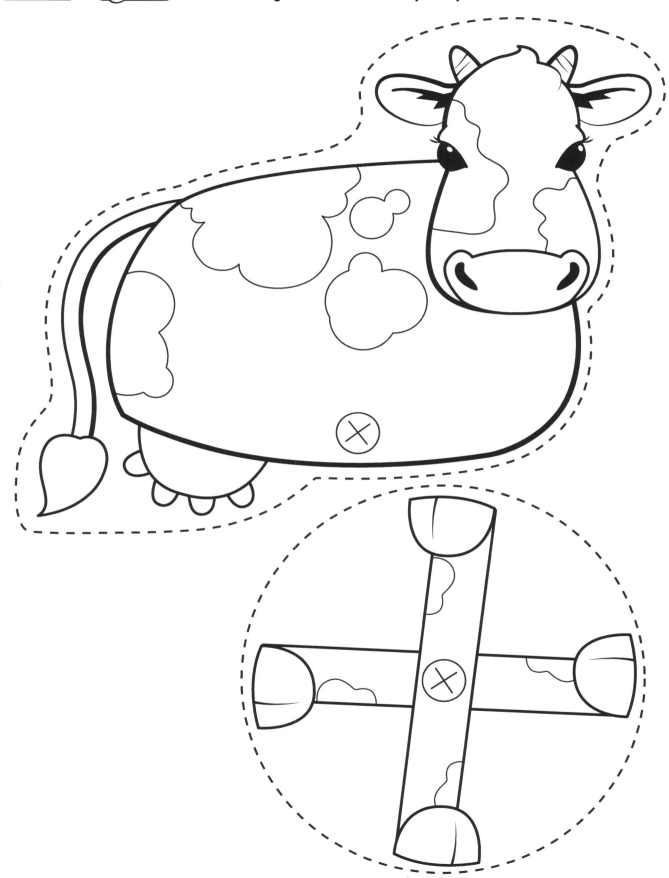

Physical sciences

What is light and where does it come from?

Content focus:	Definition, properties and sources of light
Investigative skill focus:	Questioning and predicting
	Planning and conducting
	Processing and analysing data and information
	Evaluating
	Communicating

Background information

- A definition of light is 'electromagnetic radiation to which the organs of sight react'.

- Light waves are waves of energy.

- Light waves come in many sizes. The size of a wave is measured by its wavelength (the distance between any two corresponding points on successive waves—peak-to-peak or trough-to-trough).

- Visible light is referred to as colour. We see colour in one of two ways: an object can emit light waves in the frequency of the colour we see; OR the object will absorb the frequencies of all other colours and reflect back only the light wave, or combination of light waves, that produce the colour we see.

- Light waves vibrate at different frequencies and travel at different speeds.

- Light waves can be reflected off an object, absorbed by the object, refracted through the object or pass through the object unaffected. What happens depends on the object and the energy of the light wave.

- For this age group, simple words have been used in relation to the properties of light. For example, instead of using the term 'reflect', the words 'bounces back' have been used; instead of using the term 'refract', the word 'bend' has been used. If teachers feel the pupils in their class are capable, or would enjoy learning these words in relation to properties of light, they should do so.

- Simple background information and games relating to light and dark may be found at <http://www.bbc.co.uk/schools/ks2bitesize/science/physical_processes/light_dark/read1.shtml>.

- Simple explanations about the properties of light are available at <http://www.misterteacher.com/science/light.html>. This website also provides mini-movies for interactive whiteboard viewing.

Preparation

- Introduce the topic by making the classroom as dark as possible— turn off all lights in the room and pull down all blinds/shut curtains. Allow the pupils' eyes to adjust to the darkness for a short time, then ask how it feels and what they can see. The pupils could also be asked to carefully move from one place to another in the room using a small torch for light to experience the difficulty of having little light. (Note: always ensure safety.)

The lessons

- Pages 79 and 80 should be used together.

- Read the text on page 79 with the pupils, explaining the concepts and discussing the pictures.

- Assist the pupils with answering any questions on page 80 if necessary. In particular, explain the meaning of the word 'sources' in Question 3.

- For the activity on page 81, the pupils may need to move the torch around a little to make a good rainbow.

- Places where the pupils may have seen rainbows might include in soap bubbles, near a waterfall or in mist from a hose, on the spray from waves at the beach, and in puddles of rain when oil has spilt.

Answers

Page 80

1. the sun

2. In order, the light sources are: 1 – the sun, 2 – the moon, 3 – lamp, 4 – light bulb

3. Answers will vary but should include two of the following: the light bulb, candle, fireworks, laser. Other sources given by the pupils should be discussed and accepted or rejected.

4. (a) Yes   (b) No
   (c) Yes   (d) Yes
   (e) Yes   (f) Yes

The work of scientists question
Nature and development of science/Use and influence of science

Pupils could discuss the question about conserving energy with a partner or in small groups. Ideas could include turning off lights when leaving a room; opening curtains and blinds to let in more light; reading close to a smaller wattage lamp, rather than a large room light; and changing to using energy-efficent light bulbs.

Page 81

When the narrow beam of light passes through the glass of water, a spectrum of light (a rainbow) should appear on the sheet of white paper. Light is refracted through the water in the glass, splitting up the light spectrum into colours—making a rainbow.

Physical sciences

What is light and where does it come from? – I

Read the text.

We look at and see things all the time, every day. We need light to see. But do we really know what light is?

Most of our light comes from the sun. Some objects, like our sun and often stars, give off their own light. Other things bounce back light. The moon bounces back light from the sun. It does not have its own light to give.

An insect called a firefly gives off its own light. Isn't that clever! We call the light from all these things natural light.

Other objects give artificial light. This is light created by people. Artificial light comes from things like light bulbs, candles, fireworks and lasers.

Light is a form of energy. It travels in a straight direction. It can bounce off shiny surfaces such as mirrors. It can bend when it moves from one material to another. Rainbows are made when light shines through drops of water. The drops bend the light, separating it into colours.

Light helps to keep us safe. Street lights and headlights on cars make it easier for people to see at night. Safety reflectors on bicycles and clothing bounce light so others can see us.

Light can be dangerous too. The light from the sun is very strong. When outside, it is important to protect our eyes by wearing sunglasses. Do you?

Physical sciences

What is light and where does it come from? – 2

Use the text and pictures on page 79 to complete the answers.

1. Where does most of our light come from?

_____

2. Number the sources of light in order of size.
The biggest one is number 1 and the smallest is number 4.

☐ moon   ☐ light bulb   ☐ sun   ☐ lamp

3. Draw two sources of artificial light. Write the name of each.

4. Write as yes or no.

(a) Light travels in a straight direction.   _____

(b) The moon has its own light to give.   _____

(c) A mirror bounces light.   _____

(d) Light and raindrops can make rainbows.   _____

(e) Light can bend.   _____

(f) Light can keep us safe.   _____

Scientists know what light is and how it works. We use light every day at home and school. How can we save some of the energy used to make light at home?

Make a rainbow

1. You will need:

- a glass of water (fill almost to top)
- dark room
- table
- white paper
- 2 lengths of masking tape
- torch

torch

tape

Glass almost full of water

white paper

2. Follow the steps.

(a) Place glass on edge of table.

(b) Place paper on floor close to table.

(c) Cut and place pieces of tape across end of torch so only a slit of light can shine through.

(d) Turn on torch and shine light on glass as shown in diagram.

3. Where do you think the rainbow will appear?

_____

4. Write what happened in the activity.

_____

_____

5. Did the experiment work? | Yes | No |

6. Circle the best word.

This experiment was | easy | hard |.

7. With a friend, talk about:

(a) anything that was hard to do to make the rainbow

(b) other places you have seen rainbows.

Physical sciences